THE SOUTH
DOWNS WAY

ABOUT THE AUTHOR

KEV REYNOLDS, author of this guide, is a freelance writer, photojournalist and lecturer who lives in the Kent countryside when not trekking or climbing in distant mountain regions. A prolific compiler of guidebooks, his first title for Cicerone Press appeared in 1978 (*Walks & Climbs in the Pyrenees* – now in its 4th edition); this is his 25th book for the same publisher, with others being researched at present. A member of the Alpine Club, Austrian Alpine Club and Outdoor Writers' Guild, his passion for mountains in particular and the countryside in general remains undiminished after 40 years of activity, and he regularly travels throughout Britain to share that enthusiasm through his lectures. Organisations wishing to book Kev for a lecture should write to him c/o Cicerone Press Ltd, 2 Police Square, Milnthorpe, Cumbria LA7 7PY.

THE SOUTH DOWNS WAY

by

Kev Reynolds

CICERONE PRESS
2 POLICE SQUARE, MILNTHORPE, CUMBRIA LA7 7PY
www.cicerone.co.uk

© Kev Reynolds 2001
ISBN 1 85284 324 1

First published as *The South Downs Way & The Downs Link* (1989). Revised and rewritten as *The South Downs Way* (2001).

A catalogue record for this book is available from the British Library.

Cicerone guidebooks by the same author

The North Downs Way
Walking in Sussex
Walking in Kent Vols I & II
The Wealdway & The Vanguard Way
The Cotswold Way
Walking in the Alps
100 Hut Walks in the Alps
Ecrins National Park
Walks in the Engadine – Switzerland
The Valais
The Bernese Alps
Ticino – Switzerland
Central Switzerland
The Jura (with R Brian Evans)
The Alpine Pass Route
Chamonix to Zermatt: the Walker's Haute Route
Tour of the Vanoise
Walks & Climbs in the Pyrenees
Annapurna: a Trekker's Guide
Everest: a Trekker's Guide
Langtang, Helambu & Gosainkund: a Trekker's Guide
Kangchenjunga: a Trekker's Guide
Manaslu: a Trekker's Guide

Front cover: *Alfriston's church is known as the Cathedral of the Downs (Sections 1 and 1a)*

CONTENTS

THE SOUTH DOWNS WAY

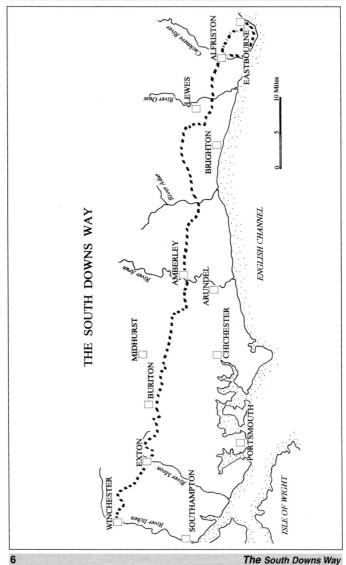

INTRODUCTION

*The start to a bright spring day…striding through a gentle downland
valley with the delightful name of Cricketing Bottom, settling into that
easy comfortable rhythm so essential to the full enjoyment of a long
walk. The early sun warm overhead, my first cuckoo of the year calling
from the hillside, the smoky haze of bluebells lining scrub-crowded
slopes where the blackthorn produces haloes of flower. Only the
pheasants complain. Larks rise singing, and all around swell the
Downs. Within less than an hour I'll be on their crest. Within that
hour I'll be wandering alone save for the peewits and skylarks and
hares, save for the cowslips at my feet and the orchids in the spin-
neys. Alone with the faintest of breezes and huge views that have the
sea gleaming in one direction, and the vast tartan plain of the Weald
in the other. Hour upon hour wandering through history, past burial
mounds and hill forts left by the first wanderers of this Way, on land
that once was covered by sea but is now serenaded day by day by
minute specks of birds whose land this really is, on grasslands grazed
by slow-moving fluffs of sheep, the close-cropped hillsides darkened
now and then by the sweeping shadows of clouds. Cloud-shadows –
the only impatience on the South Downs Way.*

A decade has passed since I first walked the South Downs Way, but I
have been back several times, drawn by the visual delights to be won
from the crest of this southern backbone of land with its over-
whelming sense of space and peace, whose trails seem to wind on
for ever – towards a dim, blue, never-to-be-reached, horizon. And
each time I tread that smooth baize of turf and look north across the
empty Weald, I find it hard to believe that this is the 'overcrowded'
South of England.

This South is a surprisingly secret land, though its secrets are there
to be unravelled if one only cares to look. It is misjudged and often
maligned, and walking through and across it is the only way properly
to discover its truths, for by wandering these ancient footpaths one
absorbs its essence through the soles of the feet. The cyclist and horse

rider will also develop an affinity with the land, but without the direct physical contact known by the walker, a unique part of the experience will be missing.

Along the South Downs Way your field of vision expands with the miles to a greater knowledge of the land. The traveller begins to appreciate that it is not so populous as is generally thought, that its countryside is infinitely more varied than might previously have been considered possible of the lowlands, and when you gain the scarp edge it is the panoramic expanse which throws into disarray any preconceived notion that mountains have a monopoly of landscape grandeur. Here the perspective fits. Scale is adjusted and beauty comes from order. In a world of constant change there is something reassuring in a vast acreage of countryside that somehow survives without too many scars – another eye-opener for the rambler in the South.

There are other surprises too, but these must be left for the wanderer, cyclist and horse rider to discover for him or herself, for along the South Downs Way any journey is bound to be full of rewards. Journeys of delight, journeys of discovery.

None but the walker can possibly understand the full extent of that statement, for it is only by the slowing of pace that one finds the ability to become part of the landscape itself. This is not something that may be achieved from the seat of a motor vehicle, for motoring divorces you from the land, and at a speed which blurs and distorts. Along country footpaths, however, there is so much to experience – from the succession of soil types beneath your feet to the *nuance* of every breeze that plays sculptor to the passing clouds. One breathes the fragrance of wayside plants, discovers the life of hedgerow and woodland shaw, and drifts through an unfolding series of panoramas. With senses finely tuned to the world about you, a footpath becomes a highway of constant discovery, of constant delight.

The Downs

In the distant mists of time, during what is known as the Cretaceous period – that is, from about 100 million to 70 million years ago – the land we now know as the Weald lay beneath the waters of a warm, shallow sea whose bed was covered by a sandwich of sedimentary deposits. Miniscule shell-bearing organisms settled on this bed, the pure calcium carbonate of their shells powdering to a chalk dust that built with staggering patience to a depth of just one foot every thirty thousand years or so. (Consider the time-scale required to produce the chalk cliffs of Beachy Head – over 500 feet/150m deep!) Yet this layer of soft crumbling chalk, composed of all these tiny shells, stretched from the Thames Valley to the Pas de Calais, and reached a depth of around 1000 feet/300m, while into this white cheese-like rock there settled also the skeletons of sea sponges to form hard seams of flint.

Then, about 20 million years ago during the Tertiary period, came the continental collision which built the Alps. Italy was thrust into Europe and Spain was pressured from the south. Mountains were slowly buckled and, as with a stone tossed into a pond, ripples spread in all directions. The chalk of southern England was raised into a huge dome rising from the sea and stretching for about 125 miles (200km), end to end. Weathering followed – a process that continues to this day. Rain, ice, frost, all combined to nibble away at this dome, aided and abetted by rivers and streams that found a weakness when the chalk cracked as it buckled. The outer edges of the dome were the last to crumble, the central core being carried away in watercourses that flowed through it. The centre of that lost dome is now the Weald, the outer edges the North and South Downs.

Rivers and streams continue to drain the Weald, breaching the Downs in valleys far broader than they now require, while dry knuckle coombs within the heart of this downland tell of streams that no longer exist.

Rambling along the smoothly rounded South Downs today we may wonder at this triumph of geological history. Gazing from the clifftop at Beachy Head we see the body of the land exposed, carved through as though with a gigantic scalpel. We gaze into the heart of unfathomable time, at the crushed, bleached remnants of creatures whose sacrifice is our gain.

East of the coastline, as the route of the South Downs Way leads away from the sea, that sacrifice is forgotten as we amble across grass-lands rich in wild flowers. Yet beneath our boots the chalk lies deep, waiting only for the plough to expose its weaknesses to the wind.

Where the path leads through arable land we see polished flints littering the fields, the chalk cushion around them turning to dust under the influence of sun and wind, ready to be brushed away. The heights of the Downs shrink in the summer breeze – one more act of sacrifice by creatures that long ago gave their shells to the southern landscape.

The common perception of the South Downs is one of rolling, flower-dazzled grasslands trimmed by sheep. This is partly due to the influence of our Neolithic ancestors who crossed from continental Europe some 5000 years ago and settled here, raising animals, clearing trees and growing crops. Until their arrival the hills would have been forested, but they, and the Iron Age settlers who arrived more than 4000 years later, cleared the forests for both agricultural purposes and for fuel, creating the open spaces that are such a feature of the eastern and central Downs today. The Romans too farmed the downland for corn, and grazed their animals on the rich meadows, but following the arrival of the Normans there was a growth in the population of villages and towns snuggling at the foot of the hills, and the number and size of flocks of downland sheep grew as a consequence. From the 14th century on the area was very heavily grazed, reaching a peak 500 years later when the eastern Sussex Downs alone supported more than 200,000 ewes and lambs. With the Second World War the nature of downland began to change once more, and in the aftermath of hostilities vast acreages were turned by the plough for the production of grain. Today the wanderer will experience a mixture of pasture, arable and woodland, a contrast that consists of meadows dancing with cowslips and the sharp golden dazzle of oil-seed rape, of yellow-headed wheat in summer and the lush foliage of beech and birchwood, of blackthorn scrub and blotches of gorse. Yet from a distance, from the low-lying Weald, the view is as Margaret Fairless Dawson (writing under the pseudonym of Michael Fairless) described it in *The Roadmender*: 'lean grey downs, keeping watch and ward between the country and the sea'.

The South Downs Way

Exploring the Sussex Downs and East Hampshire Areas of Outstanding Natural Beauty, the official South Downs Way leads for 100 miles (160km) between Eastbourne and Winchester, following the northern escarpment for much of the way and rarely descending to habitation except where river valleys interrupt the regular course of the Downs. Opened in 1972, the South Downs Way originally finished in Buriton, near the Sussex–Hampshire border, but by the end of 1987 proposals for an extension to Winchester had been approved by the Secretary of State for the Environment. However, despite protracted negotiations and a public enquiry, at the time of writing no agreement has been reached with regard to a permanent route between the Iron Age hill fort site of Old Winchester Hill, and Beacon Hill on the west side of the Meon Valley. Until such an agreement is made, the route on this section is marked as temporary – a 'temporary' solution that has so far lasted for over ten years!

The South Downs Way was the first National Trail to be developed as a bridleway throughout its entire length. In a few places the bridleway and footpath routes diverge but, apart from the initial (eastern) stage between Eastbourne and Alfriston, these are temporary alternatives only, and by far the majority of the Way is shared by ramblers, horse riders and cyclists.

Since the first edition of this guide appeared a number of improvements have been made to the Way. These include rerouting to avoid a dangerous road walk at Amberley, construction of a footbridge over the River Arun, and in two places slight diversions have been signed to afford the safe crossing of major dual carriageway roads.

For the greater part of its length the Way follows the northern crest of the South Downs escarpment, with broad views overlooking low Wealden farmlands as well as the rolling Downs. Nestling between downland hills to the south are the clefts of dry valleys, called Bottoms, or Deans. Beyond them in the eastern sector sparkles the English Channel, but further west the nature of the landscape changes and there is less a sense of height and space, and the sea is all but a memory.

Five rivers (in Sussex these are the Cuckmere, Ouse, Adur and Arun, with the lovely Meon in Hampshire) have cut valleys through the chalk, and the South Downs Way descends into – and climbs out of – them with fairly steep paths or tracks. Mostly though the route remains along the crest, sometimes on clear trackways, sometimes on flint paths, sometimes on the soft luxury of turf, and for a good

The South Downs way footpath option crosses the Seven Sisters between Eastbourne and Alfriston (Section 1)

part of the way it remains more than 650 feet (198m) above sea level. In the eastern half the Downs are open and exposed, but towards Hampshire woodlands become more frequent. Throughout, the quality of the route is first rate, with paths and gates well maintained and waymarking almost everywhere superb.

History is an ever-present companion to the route, for as we have seen the crests of the Downs were long ago used by nomadic tribes as convenient highways above the dense forests and mire of the Weald. Neolithic man began to cultivate them and to mine for the flint from which he made tools. In the Bronze and Iron Ages primitive farm sites, long barrows and hill forts began to pepper the ridges, and their tell-tale signs are there to this day – although modern farm practices have destroyed evidence of a number of these in recent years. Along the route of the South Downs Way there are something like 400 Bronze Age burial barrows. There are lynchets (ancient field systems) dating from the Iron Age rippling grass slopes where ploughed land long ago slipped against the original small field boundaries of piled stone. At Butser Hill, south of Petersfield, an Iron Age site reveals three defensive dykes, lynchets, burial mounds and ancient trackways.

During the Roman occupation routes of trade and communication were engineered across the South Downs, and so advanced were their methods of construction that some of these have been adopted as modern rights of way. In places the long-distance walker uses tracks that were laid in the first century BC, and west of Bignor Hill the South Downs Way comes to a large wooden signpost bearing directions to *Noviomagus* (Chichester) and *Londinium* (London) on the line of the Roman Stane Street built around AD 70. (Half an hour's walk away are the remains of Bignor Roman Villa, while nearer to the Way are the earthworks of a Stone Age causewayed camp.)

In valley settlements Saxon and Norman churches make a brief visit worthwhile. Along the airy crestline the trail passes numerous dew ponds created one or two hundred years ago as watering holes for the huge flocks of sheep that helped give the Downs their unique character so admired today. History, then, is all around you when you journey along the South Downs Way.

Which way to walk? West to east, or east to west? There are plenty of good reasons for arguing both directions, but since all long walks are in their essence a form of pilgrimage, Winchester makes an obvious goal and it is this ancient cathedral city that is chosen for the culmination of the South Downs Way as far as this guide is concerned.

The route begins near Beachy Head on Eastbourne's western fringe. There is an initial divergence of ways, for the bridleway heads inland via Jevington while the main footpath route goes along the clifftop of the Seven Sisters as far as Cuckmere Haven, then north on the east bank of the river valley via Westdean and Litlington to Alfriston, where it joins the bridleway.

From Alfriston the South Downs Way climbs to Bostal Hill where paragliders sail the summer skies, then on to Firle Beacon, Beddingham Hill and Iford Hill before descending from the escarpment to cross a valley cut by the River Ouse at Southease. On then to Mill Hill and Swanborough Hill, across the A27 west of Lewes, then up to Balmer Down where broad views are gained across the Weald. Ditchling Beacon is invariably busy with day trippers, the twin Clayton windmills are landmarks of genuine appeal, but beyond them there's a dip to Pyecombe on the way to the Devil's Dyke. The Way continues, keeping high to cross a series of hills, and after passing the last of these (Truleigh Hill, with its youth hostel conveniently set beside the trail), the route loses much height in order to cross the River Adur at Botolphs below Steyning.

West of the Adur Chanctonbury Ring is the major landmark, an historic circle of beech trees on an Iron Age site. The trees were badly decimated by the storm which hit southern England on 16 October 1987, but to the south, off the route but in view, is Cissbury Ring – one of the largest of all Iron Age hill fort sites. Washington lies below, alongside the busy A24, but heading west the peace of the Downs is quickly regained over Kithurst Hill, Springhead Hill and Rackham Hill, from the last of which the windings of the River Arun can be seen draining the country beyond Amberley.

A new route has been created near Amberley, and where it crosses the A29 by Coombe Wood the South Downs Way meets its midway point, marked by a signpost. The Downs now become more heavily treed and a long stretch of broad-leaved woodland accompanies the Way over Cocking Down. Pen Hill, Beacon Hill and Harting Down restore more open views, then a short woodland stretch opens along the trackway of Forty Acre Lane between South Harting and Buriton where Sussex eases into Hampshire.

Once Buriton marked the end of the walk, but it now lies a little north of the route, while the South Downs Way passes through the expanse of Queen Elizabeth Forest, where there is a possibility of sighting deer. Immediately after leaving this you climb to Butser Hill for an easy section with a far-reaching aspect. The inland naval establishment of HMS Mercury briefly interrupts the rhythm of the walk, but this soon resumes over Tegdown Hill above pretty East Meon.

More downland tracks lead to historic Old Winchester Hill, now a National Nature Reserve on the site of an Iron Age hill fort, but the bridleway (at present) misses this by making a diversion to Warnford, only rejoining the footpath route at Beacon Hill north-west of Exton. Farmland tracks and bridlepaths carry the Way on its final stage across Gander Down, Cheesefoot Head and Telegraph Hill, then into the small village of Chilcomb which is just one long field away from Winchester.

Accommodation

Although it is feasible to walk the South Downs Way in dislocated day-sections with the aid of private and/or public transport, this guide has been written primarily with the long-distance walker in mind. Accommodation along the way is therefore a prime concern. I have indicated where accommodation could be found during research, but for current details you are advised to send for a copy of the regularly updated *South Downs Way Accommodation Guide* published by, and available from, the Sussex Downs Conservation Board, whose Storrington address is given in Appendix A.

At the time of writing there are no fewer than seven youth hostels on or near the route. These are at Eastbourne, Alfriston, Telscombe, Patcham (Brighton), Truleigh Hill, Arundel and Winchester. Advanced booking is advisable as hostels can be very busy, especially during school holidays and at weekends. Full addresses and telephone numbers are given in the YHA Guide which comes free with membership – see Appendix A for the address of YHA National Office.

The Ramblers' Association also publishes details of bed and breakfast accommodation recommended by their members, and listed under county sections. This *Rambler's Yearbook and Accommodation Guide* comes free with membership and is published annually. Write to The Ramblers' Association (Appendix A).

One final source of information worth studying is *Stilwell's National Trail Companion* which lists all the main long distance trails in Britain and Ireland (including, of course, the South Downs and North Downs Ways) and provides a very useful accommodation guide. If you cannot locate a copy through your bookshop, write to Stilwell Publishing – see Appendix A.

It should be noted that there are very few recognised campsites along the Way, but should you be eager to carry a tent, it is important to gain the permission of the landowner before pitching it.

Practical Advice

One of the benefits to the walker of the South Downs Way being end-to-end bridleway is that for the vast majority of the route there are no stiles to contend with. It is only where the walker's route diverts from the bridleway that this traditionally English countryside obstacle has to be faced. Elsewhere, easy-to-open bridle gates make no demands on weary legs towards the end of a long day's walking. (If I ever make a fortune I'll replace every stile in southern England with a kissing gate!)

For the most part waymarking is exemplary (waymarks bear the white acorn symbol which indicates a National Trail), although at the western end, in Hampshire, there are one or two places where these are rather sparse and close attention to guidebook descriptions and/or reasonable map-reading skills, will prevent you from getting lost.

The route passes through one of the driest and warmest parts of the country, and for the most part bridlepaths will be firm underfoot, but following rain the bare chalk tracks soon become very slippery, which can cause problems on steep descents. Under 'normal' summer conditions there will be little mud, while exposed flints will prove uncomfortable unless you are well shod. For long periods the traveller along the South Downs Way will be fully exposed to the

*Before entering Friston Forest a fine viewpoint overlooks
the Cuckmere Valley (Section 1)*

elements with neither shelter nor shade for several miles. This *can*
create problems in summer as in winter – bright sunshine can be as
debilitating on a long walk as cold winds and rain. Be prepared for
all eventualities.

If this is your first visit to the South Downs you will be surprised
at the scarcity of villages or towns along the route – this is one of the
delights, but it can also be seen as a problem. There are occasional
country pubs for refreshment, but remarkably few shops. Fortunately
the Society of Sussex Downsmen, in conjunction with the
Countryside Commission and local authorities, has been instrumental
in providing a number of drinking-water taps for walkers and riders
along the Way. But all who tackle the route, whether on foot, bike or
horse, are advised to fill their drinking bottles at the start of each day,
and to carry food.

Getting There – and Back

Eastbourne and Winchester have good rail connections with London. Eastbourne services come from London Victoria, while those for Winchester use Waterloo. Elsewhere the South Downs Way is accessible by train with stations at Polegate, Glynde, Lewes, Hassocks and Southease. Amberley also has a station close to the route on the line to Arundel, while Petersfield, north of Buriton, has a line from London's Waterloo. Telephone numbers for railway timetable information are given in Appendix B.

For information about bus services in the area covered by this guide, readers are advised to contact the various County Council departments whose addresses are also listed in Appendix B.

Using the Guide

For the majority of the route waymarks and signposts are sufficient to make detailed guidebook descriptions superfluous. But in case doubts arise, or in the event of an occasional sign being vandalised or missing, the route is described as found on my most recent walking of it. That said, improvements are occasionally made to the Way which entail rerouting, and in such cases where waymarking differs from the description in this guide, you are advised to follow the waymarked alternative.

Notification of any major changes along the Way will be borne in mind for future editions of this book. A postcard detailing these, sent to me via the publisher, will be gratefully received.

Sketch maps included in these pages are offered as a rough guide to each stage. Placenames shown on these maps are emboldened in the text to assist navigation. The maps also show routes leading away from the South Downs Way to villages where accommodation may be found, but are no substitute for a 'proper' map, of which several are available. Perhaps the most convenient mapping of the South Downs Way is the single sheet published by Harveys at a scale of 1:40,000 (a little over 1½" = 1 mile). Printed on waterproof paper the route is shown on seven strip sections, each of which is contained within convenient folds. Additional information (in English, French and German) is provided in separate panels. The only limitation to such a map is in the restricted amount of country shown beyond the South

Downs Way 'corridor'. When you need to leave the route in search of accommodation, this map is often of little help. However, Harveys' *South Downs Way* walker's route map is well worth carrying with you.

Other maps, published by the Ordnance Survey, are mentioned at the heading of each route section to provide as great a range of options as possible. The Landranger series 1:50,000 scale (1¼" = 1 mile) should be adequate for negotiating off-route diversions for accommodation, although the Explorer series at 1:25,000 (2½" = 1 mile) gives much greater detail. However, at the time of writing neither series gives an accurate representation of the South Downs Way where recent improvements to the route have been made.

Throughout the guide additional information with regard to particularly interesting places and features seen along the Way are marked with a cross-reference number, and information is outlined at the end of each section. Where the route passes near a source of refreshment, this is mentioned.

No timings are given, but for a walk of this length an allowance of 2½ miles for each hour will probably be maintained by most regular walkers. When calculating how long any given stage is likely to take, do not forget to include rests, halts for photography, or time taken to consult the map or guidebook, all of which add substantially to the day's activity. In hot, wet or windy weather, your pace is likely to be slower than normal, so take these conditions into account too.

There is a tendency by some to rush through the countryside with one eye on the hands of the watch, and no time given for contemplation of the intricacies of the landscape, no time to absorb at leisure nature's many gifts – the pleasures that are there for all to enjoy. Walking through the countryside presents so many opportunities it would be a shame to ignore them, for there is more to walking a long-distance path than burning the miles hour after hour. If you open your eyes, heart and mind to the splendours of the world about you, you'll grow richer by the mile. So, as an antedote to the single-minded attitude of getting from A to B as quickly as possible, I've specifically written this guide with a more relaxed outlook in mind, and attempted to bring out the flavour of the walk by including a few anecdotal snippets.

The southern counties do not lend themselves to major epics, but minute by minute along the South Downs Way I experienced the wonders of the countryside. In that countryside was revealed the remarkable nature of the ordinary common scenes and pleasures that all may witness when out wandering the footpaths. Noting these little snippets that add much to the eventual sum of life's package of pleasures, it is my hope that those who follow this route will absorb as much of the landscape and the creatures that people it, as possible, and gain as much happiness as I have.

As you journey along the South Downs Way, remember it needs your care and respect.

- Guard against all risk of fire
- Fasten all gates
- Keep dogs under control
- Keep to public paths across farmland, and avoid taking short cuts which cause erosion
- Use gates and stiles to cross fences, hedges and walls
- Leave livestock, crops and machinery alone
- Take your litter home
- Help to keep all water clean
- Protect wildlife, plants and trees
- Take special care on country roads
- Make no unnecessary noise

The Country Code follows in the wake of principles set by Octavia Hill, a champion of the countryside and a co-founder of the National Trust , who wrote in the early days of the 20th century:

> *'Let the grass growing for hay be respected, let the primrose roots be left in their loveliness in the hedges, the birds unmolested and the gates shut. If those who frequented country places would consider those who live there, they would better deserve, and more often retain, the rights and privileges they enjoy.'*

SECTION 1: EASTBOURNE TO ALFRISTON
(Footpath route via the Seven Sisters)

Distance:	10½ miles (17km)
Maps:	Harveys South Downs Way 1:40,000
	OS Landranger 199 Eastbourne, Hastings & Surrounding Area 1:50,000
	OS Explorer 123 South Downs Way, Newhaven to Eastbourne 1:25,000
Accommodation:	Eastbourne, Birling Gap, Foxhole and Alfriston
Refreshments:	Eastbourne, Beachy Head, Birling Gap, Exceat, Litlington, Alfriston

Of the two primary stages leading to Alfriston, this route across Beachy Head and the Seven Sisters is not a dedicated bridleway, but is the official walkers' route – the bridleway alternative goes inland via Jevington, and is described as Section 1(a) below. It is difficult to say which is the finer option for both have much to commend them. So good are the two options, in fact, that it is tempting to walk each one in due course. The clifftop region of Heritage Coast above Eastbourne is scenically dramatic, for the surf froths far below and as you wander across Beachy Head you have a lovely view ahead to the Seven Sisters, with Seaford Head beyond the estuary of Cuckmere Haven. The inland route, on the other hand, makes a splendid introduction to the Downs with wide open vistas almost every step of the way, while the little community of Jevington visited mid-journey is a typical flint-walled village with an attractive church in gentle surroundings.

The official route begins on the south-western edge of Eastbourne at Holywell. It then mounts steep, scrub-covered slopes

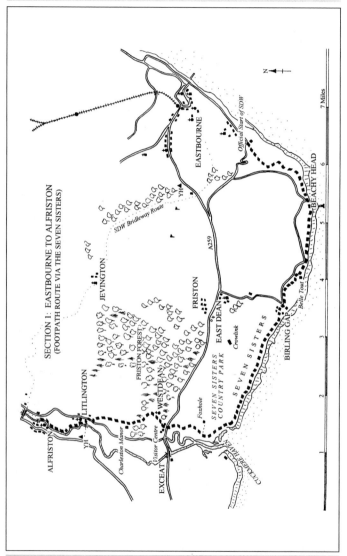

SECTION 1: EASTBOURNE TO ALFRISTON
(FOOTPATH ROUTE VIA THE SEVEN SISTERS)

to Beachy Head, continues across to Birling Gap and then tackles the rise and fall of the Seven Sisters. After leaving Haven Brow, the last of the 'Sisters', the route descends gently to the east bank of the Cuckmere, before cutting off and rising once more, this time over sheep-grazed downland to the site of the former Exceat church, then down to the A259 near the Seven Sisters Visitor Centre. A steep hillside leads to Friston Forest where a fine view shows the lazy windings of the Cuckmere below. Westdean is briefly visited, then it's back to forest again. But once the trees have been left behind high farmland takes the route down to Litlington and the banks of the Cuckmere, which makes a gentle companion for the final approach to Alfriston.

Intro 1: To reach the start of the South Downs Way from **Eastbourne**[1] railway station, walk along Grove Road passing the Town Hall, and follow Meads Road through the Meads area of town. At the junction of Beachy Head Road take Meads Street which leads past shops and eventually brings you to King Edward's Parade. The walk begins where Dukes Drive makes a sharp right-hand bend. A refreshment kiosk is seen to the left (Grid ref: 600972).

Intro 2: To reach the start of the South Downs Way from the promenade, head south away from Eastbourne pier with the sea to your left, walking towards the stumpy martello tower[2] known as the Wish Tower. Beyond it there are neat lawns and flower beds. The promenade continues towards the cliffs, and as the path rises and brings you to a large landscaped mound with seats, bear right to King Edward's Parade. Turn left to Holywell, and when Dukes Drive bends sharply to the right, you see the start of the South Downs Way directly ahead (Grid ref: 600972).

Start: At first the Way climbs a steep slope of grass and scrub, then up a flight of concrete steps to a junction of paths. Take the left-hand option among more scrub and gorse, coming out to an open downland above the rim of Whitbread Hole and its playing field. The continuing path winds among bushes of blackthorn, gorse and elder and then, climbing steadily on an old coastguard's path and with splendid views over the sea, approaches **Beachy Head**.[3] (*Refreshments at the nearby Beachy Head Inn.*)

Continue along the clifftop, but do not stray too close to the edge as the cliffs are crumbling. The way slopes down almost to road level below the former lighthouse of **Belle Tout**,[4] then rises to pass round the inland side of the enclosing wall. Maintain direction across the cliffs, which were acquired by the National Trust in 1967 and form a designated Heritage Coast, and from which the Seven Sisters can be seen ahead. Before long you arrive at the few buildings and car park at **Birling Gap** (*accommodation, refreshments*) (Grid ref: 554960).

I was glad then to have chosen to walk westwards, for although the sky was bright and clear, a cold easterly wind was blowing, and I'd rather have that in my back than in my face all day long. On the clifftop walk tiny cowslips were coming into bloom, but few other flowers as yet. Later, and further inland, there would be plenty of colour around my boots, but up here I was well content with views over the sea, with the bleached helter-skelter of the Seven Sisters ahead with their thatch of downland grass, trim and neatly cropped, and recalled previous clifftop wanderings at the end of a variety of long walks. The pleasure to be gained whilst wandering across the Seven Sisters never palls. There's the cry of gulls, the sight, scent and sound of the sea, and broad vistas of the Downs stretching far away inland. I had the wind in my hair and a hundred miles to cover at my own pace. It was good to be back.

A flint track heads past what appears to be a tarred cottage (but is, in fact, a toilet block), then soon forks. The way ahead leads to East Dean, but we veer left and through a gate rejoin the clifftop path. The route now wanders over the **Seven Sisters** on a switchback course with the sea glistening below to the left and the green baize of the Downs spreading far off to the right – the Crowlink estate owned by the National Trust. On the first of the 'Sisters' an obelisk records the dedication of land to the Trust in memory of two brothers killed in the First World War. Next is Bailey's Hill, followed by Flat Hill, Flagstaff Brow (another dedication stone), Brass Point, Rough Brow, Short Brow and Haven Brow. Between the 'Sisters' steep, dry valleys, or 'bottoms' can be testing for legs and knees, and the red faces of other walkers betray the effort of each ascent.

From Haven Brow a clear view shows Cuckmere Haven[5] below, with Seaford Head on the far side. The way slopes down and curves to the right, and on reaching the valley bed, goes through a gate and onto a chalk path, the Cuckmere River just to the left. Immediately after crossing a concrete farm road go through a kissing gate and walk up the slope ahead in a north-easterly direction.

Note: *For camping, or simple camping barn accommodation at* **Foxhole** *follow the concrete farm road to the right.*

There is little visible sign of a path, but low waymark posts direct the way to another gate on what is almost the highest point. Through this you approach a stone marking the site of the 11th century church of Exceat, although there's nothing of the building to be seen. The way now veers a little leftwards heading north-west where a clear path will be found cutting round the hillside above the Cuckmere's windings, then angles gently down to a gate opposite the Seven Sisters Visitor Centre[6] (*refreshments*) (Grid ref: 519995).

Cross the A259 with care and wander between a cycle hire building and a cottage, then through a kissing gate and up a steep grass slope, at the top of which a stone stile leads through a wall to the edge of Friston Forest.[7] There's a very fine view from here, out to the Cuckmere's valley easing towards Cuckmere Haven. Take the path ahead among trees, and soon descend more than 200 steps to the hamlet of **Westdean**[8] which is reached beside an attractive duck

The Old Rectory in Westdean, an attractive village on the way to Alfriston

pond. Continue ahead along a narrow road which becomes a track, and re-enter Friston Forest. Waymarks direct the South Downs Way to the left, but on coming to a junction of tracks, turn right, and when this bears sharp right near the forest edge, the way goes ahead and descends more steps among trees behind **Charleston Manor**.[9]

The South Downs Way continues along a beech-lined track, then you veer right to cross a stile and follow a hedge. (On the downland slopes to the west, a white horse can be seen cut in the chalk above the Cuckmere Valley, on the hill known as High and Over.) Eventually come down to the flint-walled village of **Litlington**[10] (*refreshments*). Turn right in the village street as far as *The Plough and Harrow* pub. Just beyond this turn left along a narrow footpath leading to a bridge over the Cuckmere.

Note: *If you plan to stay overnight at **Alfriston Youth Hostel**, cross the river here, go up the slope beyond and the hostel is on the right, beside the road (☎ 01323 870423).*

The continuing South Downs Way turns right and follows the Cuckmere upstream, passing opposite the Clergy House and Alfriston parish church, to a bridge with white railings where the footpath route joins the bridleway (Grid ref: 523031). Cross the bridge and walk ahead up an alleyway which brings you directly into **Alfriston** High Street (*refreshments, accommodation*) where you turn right to *The Star Inn*.

Alfriston is something of a show-piece village, and is one of the busiest in all of Sussex with day-visitors. It boasts many interesting and picturesque buildings, a number of which have typical downland flint walls. The George Inn (built 1397) is said to have been a smuggler's haunt, while The Star Inn, which dates from the 15th century, bears the figurehead of a Dutch ship that foundered in Cuckmere Haven. The 14th century church of St Andrew, standing between the greensward of The Tye and the Cuckmere River, is often referred to as 'the Cathedral of the Downs'. Nearby the thatched, half-timbered Clergy House is of similar age to the church, and was the first building bought (in 1896) by the National Trust – for just £10! Alfriston has several shops, restaurants, pubs and tearooms, and a choice of accommodation.

Eastbourne Youth Hostel, located near the bridleway to Alfriston

Items of Interest

1: Eastbourne is one of those South Coast resorts that has retained an air of gentility. It's a town of flower beds and bowling greens, a town where Victorian imagery lingers on. The original settlement of East Bourne had á church before the Norman invasion. There were neighbouring hamlets called South Bourne and Sea Houses, the latter a collection of fishermen's cottages, but the three were amalgamated in the mid-19th century, and in 1910 Eastbourne was created a borough. Development as a resort was due largely to the seventh Duke of Devonshire, and it has somehow managed to avoid the tackiness of so many of its coastal neighbours, and discreetly shuns vulgarity. Along the front north of the pier stands The Redoubt, a sturdy, circular building – mostly of brick – constructed in the early 1800s as part of the coastal defences against Napoleon. The Wish Tower (see below) also formed part of that defence system. (Tourist Information Centre: Cornfield Road, Eastbourne BN21 4LQ ☎ 01323 411400.)

2: The Martello Tower, known as the Wish Tower, is the sole survivor of four such towers originally built along Eastbourne's seafront in 1806/7 in order to keep Napoleon at bay. During the Napoleonic Wars a whole series of these stocky circular towers were erected along the coastline of Kent and Sussex, and named after the Torre del Martello in Napoleon's homeland of Corsica.

3: Beachy Head is one of the best-known features of the Sussex coast. The clifftop is 536 feet (163m) above the waves, while the red and white ringed lighthouse at its base was built in 1902, the builders and the stone being lowered from the clifftop by cableway. At the start of 1999 a massive rockfall destroyed a section of cliff-face at Beachy Head – a not-so-subtle warning to avoid straying too near the edge.

4: Belle Tout lighthouse predates that of Beachy Head. Built in 1831 of Aberdeen granite by Mad Jack Fuller, the eccentric squire of Brightling, it served as the lighthouse for this stretch of coast until 1901, but was replaced because the light would often be lost in fog. It has now been converted to a private dwelling, and following the Beachy Head cliff-fall in 1999, Belle Tout was physically moved a short distance inland.

5: Cuckmere Haven is the estuary of the Cuckmere River, a shingle bank guarded by Haven Brow and Seaford Head. In the 15th century it was more open than it is today, for in 1460 raiders from France sailed up the river to Exceat and attacked the village. (Exceat barely exists as a village today.) During the 18th century the Haven was a notorious landing place for smugglers, when contraband goods would be brought upstream to Exceat and Alfriston. As recently as 1923 smugglers were caught there with a haul of expensive brandy. A little inland from the Haven itself a man-made lagoon attracts assorted waders, while the snaking Cuckmere between Exceat and the Haven is busy with swans, tufted ducks, dabchicks, cormorants and herons.

6: The Seven Sisters Country Park spreads east of the River Cuckmere and covers an area of 690 acres. Established in 1971 by East Sussex County Council, but managed by the Sussex Downs Conservation

Board, the Visitor Centre is housed in a converted 18th century barn at Exceat. The Centre has an interesting wildlife and local history exhibition, a shop and toilets. Next door is a convenient restaurant.

7: Friston Forest covers almost 2000 acres of mainly broad-leaved woodlands. It is owned by South East Water, but managed by the Forestry Commission, and there are several paths and rides through it.

8: Westdean is a historic little place. It is said that Alfred the Great built a palace here in AD 850, although no trace of it has been found. But there is a charming flint-built rectory dating from the 13th century, and a part-Norman church nearby. Although very small, and with an air of seclusion, Westdean is worth exploring at leisure.

9: Charleston Manor on the edge of Friston Forest is named in the Domesday Book as being owned by William the Conqueror's cup-bearer, Cerlestone. In the grounds the restored tithe barn is all of 177 feet (54m) long, with an enormous tiled roof and a medieval circular dovecote. The gardens are open to the public on set days during the summer.

10: Litlington is tucked under the Downs on the east bank of the Cuckmere, its small Norman church wearing a white weatherboarded bell-tower and a shingled cap. Nextdoor Church Farm is also very old, and has Caen stone in its walls which leads some to suggest it may have been a Priest's House. The name of the village is derived from 'Lytela's farmstead' and is pronounced Lillington.

SECTION 1(a): EASTBOURNE TO ALFRISTON
(Bridleway route inland via Jevington)

Distance:	7½ miles (12km)
Maps:	Harveys South Downs Way 1:40,000
	OS Landranger 199 Eastbourne, Hastings & Surrounding Area 1:50,000
	OS Explorer 123 South Downs Way, Newhaven to Eastbourne 1:25,000
Accommodation:	Eastbourne, Jevington, Wilmington (+ 1 mile), Alfriston
Refreshments:	Eastbourne, Jevington, Alfriston

The bridleway alternative to the Seven Sisters route is a delightful stage among rolling downland which affords wide views and with plenty of interest throughout. In many respects it is as rewarding as the official footpath stage described above, albeit of a completely different nature, and is highly recommended. As with the Seven Sisters route it begins in a low-key way, with no hint of the delights to come, no suggestion that ahead lies a journey of countless scenic pleasures. But these steadily unfold within the first mile or so, for once on the route proper, the Way emerges onto the Downs near a golf course overlooking Eastbourne and the distant Pevensey Levels, and heads north before descending a clear track among gorse bushes and banks of wild flowers, into a narrow valley with Jevington neatly spaced within its confines. A tree-shaded climb leads onto the Downs again, and at Windover Hill the route journeys across the unseen head of England's largest chalk figure, the Long Man of Wilmington. More expansive views entice across the Cuckmere's gap towards Bostal Hill and Firle Beacon, and northward into the flat open spaces of the Weald. A winding chalk track snakes down to the Cuckmere's valley, then

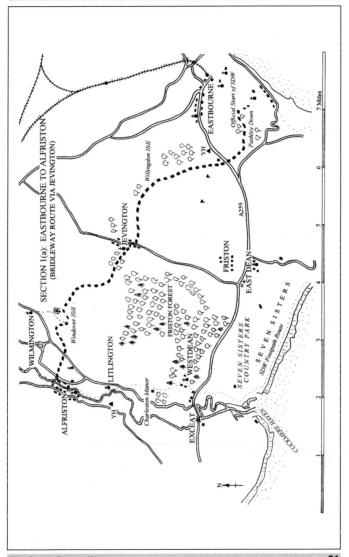

SECTION 1(a): EASTBOURNE TO ALFRISTON
(BRIDLEWAY ROUTE VIA JEVINGTON)

the bridleway edges water-meadows before joining the footpath route for a crossing of the Cuckmere into Alfriston.

Intro 1: The bridleway begins in Paradise Drive, a short distance to the south-west of **Eastbourne** railway station. To reach the start from the station, walk south along Grove Road, and continue along Meads Road until reaching Carlisle Road which crosses it. Turn right and before long you'll see Paradise Drive curving to the right. A short distance along this the South Downs Way cuts off on the left, on a rising track (Grid ref: 598982).

Intro 2: To reach the start of the South Downs Way from the promenade, facing Eastbourne pier turn right and soon passing Wish Tower (a stumpy martello tower) continue among neat lawns and flower beds, rising then to a large landscaped mound with seats. Bear right to King Edward's Parade and cross over into Chesterfield Road, a residential street. At the far end bear right and continue along Milnthorpe Road, straight over St Johns Road and Meads Road just beyond that, and ahead on Gaudick Road. At the end of this go slightly left ahead into Paradise Drive. Just after Link Road breaks away, the SDW track can be seen cutting off to the left (Grid ref: 598982).

Intro 3: Horse riders may find it easier to un-box at Warren Hill car park, and begin there. The car park is found at the south-western end of town where Dukes Drive (B2103) rises towards its junction with A259 (Grid ref: 587979). A bridleway strikes away from the car park heading north-east, and very shortly joins the main South Downs Way bridlepath on **Pashley Down** a short distance before the Way crosses the A259 near the golf course.

Start: A noticeboard formerly stood here to announce the beginning of the South Downs Way, but waymarks (blue arrows bearing the white acorn symbol) indicate the route. The track rises easily alongside a narrow belt of woodland. Hidden among the trees a short distance up the slope is an underground reservoir, but this will only be seen if you look seriously for it. You soon gain views of the sea to the left and, passing scrub, come onto the summit of the hill where there is an obelisk trig point just left of the bridleway. Beyond this the way veers right and joins another grass track – the bridleway alterna-

The Cuckmere River writhes its way to Cuckmere Haven (Section 1)

Postbox in Westdean set in a wall of local Downland flint (Section 1)

St Andrew's, Jevington, has a Saxon tower 1000 years old (Section 1a)

tive from Warren Hill car park. With Eastbourne seen sprawling below to the right, follow a fenceline to the A259 road (Grid ref: 585985).

Note: *Eastbourne Youth Hostel is situated about a third of a mile downhill to the right, in a converted golf clubhouse (☎ 01323 721081).*

Cross the road with care and take the broad track opposite, through a golf course. The track is easy to follow and it leads for a little over 2½ miles (4km) to Jevington. There are fine views almost all the way. At first these extend across the low-lying Pevensey Levels to the right, while to the left East Dean sprawls in its hollow, with Friston water tower projecting thumb-like above it. The way passes a dew pond,[1] and ¾ mile later comes to cross-tracks at **Willingdon Hill** (Grid ref: 577009). Just above to the right is a trig point, and on the mound which marks the crown of the hill there once stood a windmill. Note the stone marker which mentions Old Town Eastbourne and Jevington – it came from Barclays Bank whose Eastbourne building was bombed during the last war. The right-hand track here is the route of the Wealdway.[2]

Ignoring alternatives to right and left continue ahead, now descending beside clumps of gorse on what becomes a delightful sunken track with a preview of Jevington snug in its valley below. The banks are lavish with flowers in springtime – cowslips,[3] bugle, and wild raspberry canes straggling by the fence.

A luxurious fold of downland spread in gentle curves on all sides. Pausing to take it all in I recognised the shape of Combe Hill to the north where I had crossed one glorious late-spring afternoon a couple of years ago when walking the Wealdway. I remembered it well: the peace, the views, the sunshine. Now I had the peace of a spring morning, more fine views and sunshine too. Ahead, Jevington sank into a crease of hills. Behind it a sloping meadow on the Downs had recently been rolled in stripes, as though a welcome carpet had been laid out for my arrival. In one such meadow horses were grazing. In another the lazy drift of sheep shuffled patterns of white on green. Happiness, I thought, is something we're seldom aware of until it has passed. But wandering down the track towards Jevington with the sun

*on my neck, I knew there was nowhere else I'd rather be, and
nothing I'd rather be doing than setting off on a hundred-mile
walk across those Downs. Ambling down the track to Jevington,
I was happy. And knew it.*

On reaching **Jevington**[4] (*accommodation, refreshments*) turn right
along the road and about 50 yards later bear left on the approach to
the church. Continue beyond the Saxon church of St Andrew along a
narrowing enclosed bridleway where a signpost indicates Alfriston 3
miles. Soon the way rises among horse chestnut, elm, ash and elder,
crosses another track and shortly joins a more prominent path which
continues up the slope – beside which wild garlic and bluebells mass
in springtime. At Holt Brow emerge from trees to a crossing path.
Turn right and within a few yards go through a bridle gate. Maintain
direction along the edge of a field, and through a second gate come
to a large open grassland.

There is a sudden awareness of space as you emerge onto the
bare crest of the Downs. There are far views to the sea, but much
closer downland folds into the green coomb of Deep Dean. The
ruined walls of Hill Barn give rise to speculation as to their origin.

Several low waymark posts guide the route across this downland
plateau before a clear chalk path leads along the top edge of Deep
Dean to another gate (Grid ref: 544034). Passing through, veer left.
The lip of the escarpment is now to your right, and should you venture
to it you notice Wilmington[5] far below, Arlington Reservoir beyond
that and the immense levels of the Weald spreading to a distant blue
line of Ashdown Forest. Although you will not see it from this point,
you are virtually standing on the head of the Long Man of
Wilmington. The Cuckmere River snakes out of the Weald, and to the
west you gaze across the broad valley it has cut through the Downs,
to the rise of Bostal Hill and Firle Beacon where the South Downs
Way passes on Section 2.

Now heading south-west the grassy trail passes along the left-
hand side of various earthworks on **Windover Hill** (two or three burial
barrows and ditches, and mounds that indicate refuse pits from Stone
Age flint mines.) Beyond the summit of Windover Hill the route winds
to the right and then left, descending a sunken track, formerly a coach
road, round the head of another dry valley (Ewe Dean).

Note: *If you plan to find accommodation in* **Wilmington**, *take the right-hand option when the track forks. At crosstracks turn right on a path which cuts along the flank of hillside to the foot of the Long Man. Now bear left on an enclosed path which leads to a narrow lane. Bear right into Wilmington.*

The track takes you past an underground reservoir and eventually spills onto a country lane. Cross straight over and continue down a narrow sunken track among blackthorn and a line of elms, until coming to a road junction. Cross slightly left ahead and enter a meadow, then turn left and remaining parallel with the road keep along the edge of the meadow with Alfriston church seen ahead, the Cuckmere off to the right hidden below a grass embankment. At the end of the meadow go through a gate and turn right along a metalled path. As you come to a white-railed footbridge you join the footpath route from the Seven Sisters. On the **Alfriston** side of the bridge the bridleway bears right in front of cottages, then left between flint walls to reach the Market Cross in the High Street (*accommodation, refreshments*) (Grid ref: 520032). Now head to the left along the street as far as the *The Star Inn.*

Note: *For information about* **Alfriston**, *please refer to the end of Section 1, Footpath Route.*

Items of Interest:

1: Dew Ponds are seen in many parts of the South Downs. Because of the permeable nature of chalk, there is practically no natural surface water, so saucer-shaped scoops have been dug out and in many places given a concrete base (clay was originally used) to trap and contain rainwater for grazing animals. Traditionally these dew ponds were known as 'cloud ponds', 'mist ponds' or, more prosaically, 'sheep ponds'.

2: The Wealdway is a long-distance recreational route which travels 82 miles (132km) from the bank of the River Thames at Gravesend in Kent, to the clifftop at Beachy Head. On the way it crosses the North Downs, several High Weald ridges, Ashdown Forest, the expanse of the Weald and, finally, the South Downs. See *The Wealdway & The Vanguard Way* by Kev Reynolds (Cicerone Press).

3: Cowslips are symbolic of the Downs, and these lovely yellow-headed plants will be seen in abundance throughout the walk in late springtime. The name originates from the belief that the flower would appear wherever there was a cowpat! For centuries it was used as an ingredient in the making of vinegar, mead, wine and even cheese.

4: Jevington is a quiet, back-country downland village that was once a smugglers' haunt. The flint-walled church of St Andrew has an impressive Saxon tower 1000 years old, in which there is a bell said to have been brought ashore from a shipwreck. The remainder of the building dates from the 13th century, but there are Roman bricks in its construction. *The Hungry Monk* restaurant opposite the lane leading to the church is where the Banoffee Pie was invented in 1972!

5: Wilmington is famous for The Long Man, said to be England's largest chalk figure, which stands 226 feet (69m) long and, with a stave in each hand, overlooks the ruins of a Benedictine priory founded in 1100. No-one knows quite how old the Long Man is although it has been suggested that he dates from the Bronze Age, about 4000 years ago. Both he and the priory ruins are now in the care of the Sussex Archaeological Trust. The parish church next door to the priory has a weatherboarded bell-tower topped with a shingle spire, and is as old as the priory, while an enormous yew tree in the churchyard is thought to be 1600 years old. The pendulous branches are supported by wooden props and chains.

SECTION 2: ALFRISTON TO SOUTHEASE

Distance:	7 miles (11km)
Maps:	Harveys South Downs Way 1:40,000
	OS Landranger 199 Eastbourne, Hastings & Surrounding Area and 198 Brighton & The Downs 1:50,000
	OS Explorer 123 South Downs Way, Newhaven to Eastbourne and 122 South Downs Way, Steyning to Newhaven 1:25,000
Accommodation:	West Firle (+ 1 mile), Rodmell, Telscombe Hostel (+ 1¼ miles)
Refreshments:	None on the route, other than a drinking-water tap at Southease.

This section mounts to the northern crest of the Downs for a lovely walk on smooth grass speckled with flowers, among sites of ancient history where long barrows roughen the turf, and where a remote Saxon cemetery holds the secrets of a past age remote from the technology of the 21st century. From Alfriston's busy heart the route climbs to Bostal Hill where the summer skies are bright with multi-coloured paragliders. Then on to Firle Beacon, 713 feet (217m) above the sea, whose crown has been cropped by genera- tions of Southdown sheep. The Downs then curve westward, and the trail crosses Beddingham Hill beside a pair of lofty radio masts to reach Itford Hill overlooking the River Ouse. A winding descent comes to Itford Farm and the Newhaven road, and once across the river you enter the tiny village of Southease. For accommodation in either Rodmell or Telscombe it is necessary to continue a little beyond the village.

Since there is no certainty of refreshment on this section of the walk (on occasion drinks may be available near Itford Farm), it is advisable to carry supplies from Alfriston.

The South Downs Way goes along the narrow street beside *The Star Inn*, over a crossing road and ahead into Kings Ride, a residential street. At the head of this a flint and chalk track rises gently. Ignore alternative routes breaking to the right until, towards the top of the slope, the track forks. Take the right-hand option which crosses another track a few paces later. Continue ahead, making for the crown of **Bostal Hill**, and passing on the way a hidden long barrow (Long Burgh), a Saxon burial ground, and several other tumuli. Once atop the Downs a huge vista includes the sea far out to the left, but behind, looking back on the previous section of the route, the Long Man of Wilmington is hidden from view, but the rolling downland wall is clearly seen above both Wilmington and Alfriston, stretching southward to Cuckmere Haven. The Weald is a low-lying contrast with Berwick (a neat corner worth searching out on another occasion), huddled in an expanse of green.

> *Striding towards Bostal Hill my attention was caught by what appeared to be a mass of giant butterflies drifting in the breeze, but on drawing closer revealed themselves to be paragliders, each brightly-coloured arc of silk supporting a speck of man or woman competing with the larks for a privileged overview of the Downs and the Weald. I counted seventeen in all, spiralling, drifting, soaring – hanging in the sky and connected with the earth only by their shadows.*

Across Bostal Hill the trail comes to a small car park, and beyond this maintains direction for ¾ mile to **Firle Beacon**, which is marked by a trig point from which there's another immense panorama to enjoy (Grid ref: 485059).

Note: *Just beyond the trig point an alternative path descends to* **West Firle** *(or Firle as it is known), and is the one to take if you plan to find accommodation there.*

The Way now curves westward aiming towards lofty radio masts on **Beddingham Hill** nearly two miles away – as the route passes below them they form a convenient marker. Between Firle Beacon

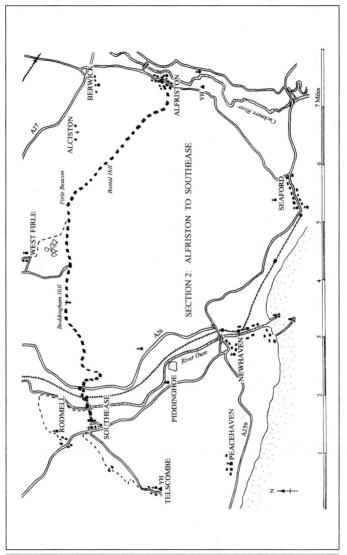

SECTION 2: ALFRISTON TO SOUTHEASE

and the radio masts the way goes through another small car park, this one giving road access to Firle[1] seen at the foot of the Downs.

Around us now are more prehistoric sites – round barrows and ancient settlements. There was an Iron Age village near Firle Beacon, a Bronze Age collection of huts and workshops west of Beddingham Hill. North of the escarpment, and on the outskirts of Glynde, there was an Iron Age hill fort on Mount Caburn. For more than 300 years it was occupied and active, until the Romans came. Roman track-ways crossed the Downs above Firle as part of an important trade route. Grain would have been carted along these tracks bound for the coast where Seaford and Newhaven stand today. On these Downs, 'broad and bare to the skies', only a handful of modern cars, a few model aircraft and the twin radio masts ahead represent a world so very different to that experienced by the first settlers of these green sweeping crests. Yet with imagination it is possible to stir the spirits of our windblown ancestors, and share with them the empty miles.

Pass along the right-hand side of the masts. The track then veers a little to the right and goes through a gate by a narrow metalled road. Cross through another gate directly ahead and wander parallel with the left-hand fence towards Itford Hill, eventually passing a trig point and a dried-up dew pond known as Red Lion Pond on your right (Grid ref: 446055).

From here to the valley of the Ouse the downland is rich in wild flowers, with views stretching from Newhaven out to the left where the Ouse spills into the sea, to Lewes and Mount Caburn off to the right. On reaching the lip of the Downs, Itford Farm is seen below to the west, beside the A26. The slope plunges steeply, but the way swings left across the slope as far as a farm track. Now follow this downhill beside banks of cowslips in spring, and come to the A26 Lewes to Newhaven road. Bear right, and after about 100 yards cross the road with caution, and follow the lane opposite which takes you past Itford Farm.

Note: *There is a water point and horse trough beside the lane. On occasion the cottage behind the water point advertises refreshments for sale.*

The lane crosses the railway line at the halt of Southease station, then a short distance beyond comes to the River Ouse. This is contained between sturdy banks, and is crossed by road bridge. The reedy ditches beyond form a lively habitat for frogs and toads, and heron are sometimes seen stalking for a meal.

Note: *The main South Downs Way continues along the lane into Southease, but an optional alternative which misses the hamlet, visits Rodmell instead and would be useful for anyone planning to spend the night there (although there is a shorter and more direct road route to Rodmell mentioned in Section 3 below). Take the riverside path on the right immediately after crossing the bridge and walk downstream for about a mile. On coming to a track (bridleway) turn left and follow this into* **Rodmell**.[2] *To rejoin the South Downs Way walk along Mill Lane, which starts from the main road near the Abergavenny Arms, initially between cottages. The lane narrows and becomes a private road (but public bridleway) with fields on the left folding down into Cricketing Bottom. Near the crest of the hill, by the entrance to Mill Hill (Grid ref: 413054), turn right on an enclosed bridleway running parallel with the garden boundary. This is the route of the South Downs Way.*

Keep on the lane, and about 400 yards beyond the bridge you enter the hamlet of **Southease** near the village green.

Note: *If you plan to spend the night at* **Telscombe Youth Hostel** *follow directions given in Section 3: Southease to Housedean.*

Southease consists of a few 17th century cottages, a village green and an attractive church with a rare circular tower built in the 12th century (there are only three such towers in Sussex, all of which are in the Ouse valley), and some faded, medieval wall paintings. Southease was first recorded in a charter of AD 966 granting the church and manor – and that of nearby Telscombe – to Hyde Abbey in Winchester. Southease was then 'Sueise' and the charter, made by the Anglo-Saxon King Edgar (Eadgar), included 28 hides of land. In the Domesday Book of 1086 the village rated 27 hides and 'the villeins are assessed for 38,500 herrings and at £4 for porpoises.' This reference to herrings and porpoises gives an indication of the importance of Southease as a fishery. At the time the Ouse was a major tidal river, and it is thought possible that the lake in the grounds of Southease Place may have once been a harbour.

Items of Interest:

1: Firle, shown as West Firle on OS maps, is a compact village nestling below the Downs. The elegant Firle Place, which stands near the church with a woodland behind, was originally built in 1557, but then rebuilt nearly 200 years later – the Georgian outer retaining the Tudor core. To the east of Firle Place stands the round folly of Firle Tower, which is clearly seen from the Downs near Firle Beacon. Charleston Farmhouse, further east again, became a centre for the Bloomsbury Group of writers and artists after being discovered in 1916 by Virginia and Leonard Woolf. The house now contains work by Virginia's sister, Vanessa Bell, and Duncan Grant who died in 1978.

2: Rodmell is best known for Monks House, the home of Virginia and Leonard Woolf (see above), which is now in the ownership of the National Trust. They came here in 1919, but in 1941 Virginia, suffering mental illness, walked down to the River Ouse and committed suicide. Rodmell has a Norman church and some attractive cottages. South-west of the village, on the route of the South Downs Way there used to stand a windmill, and the Abergavenny Arms pub beside the main road is named after the Marquess of Abergavenny who, until just after the First World War, was the principal landowner.

SECTION 3: SOUTHEASE TO HOUSEDEAN (A27)

Distance:	**6 miles (9½km)**
Maps:	**Harveys South Downs Way 1:40,000**
	OS Landranger 198 Brighton & The Downs 1:50,000
	OS Explorer 122 South Downs Way, Steyning to Newhaven 1:25,000
Accommodation:	**Rodmell (+ ½ mile), Telscombe Youth Hostel (+ 1¼ miles), Lewes (+ 1½–2 miles)**
Refreshments:	**None on the route**

This section of the South Downs Way was improved in two places in 1995, thanks to the Sussex Downs Conservation Board, taking the route off the road just outside Southease (which, incidentally, makes it easier to reach Telscombe YH for accommodation), and at the end of the stage where the Way formerly made a hazardous crossing of the A27 to the west of Lewes, a diversion has been created which now leads the SDW over a convenient bridge.

On this section the route journeys over another broad, exposed downland ridge heading north-west over Mill Hill, Front Hill, Iford Hill (not to be confused with Itford Hill of the last section), then along the scarp edge of Swanborough Hill overlooking neat villages tucked against the foot of the Downs. There are more dew ponds, the site of a one-time windmill, and a stretch along Juggs Road, a track formerly used by fish traders travelling from Brighton to Lewes. Brighton is kept at bay well to the west as the South Downs Way curves round the head of Cold Coombes then descends alongside Newmarket Plantation to the A27. Once across this busy road, walkers seeking accommodation could catch a bus into Lewes.

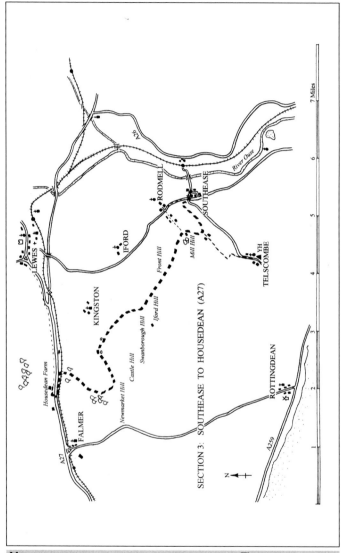

SECTION 3: SOUTHEASE TO HOUSEDEAN (A27)

On a calm and sunny day this makes a gorgeous walk. Larks rise from the fields to trill overhead. There will, no doubt, be pheasants and hares sharing the track; there are badger setts along Swanborough Hill, foxes in Newmarket Plantation, and wild flowers set in the downland turf. There are no refreshment facilities at all along the way, and no habitation between Mill Hill and the A27. But views there are in plenty.

Passing Southease church on your left walk up the tree-lined lane to a road junction where you turn right. After a few paces another lane cuts left, signposted to Telscombe. At the entrance to this lane you will find a gate on the northern side leading into a meadow.

Note: *If you need accommodation in **Rodmell** do not go through this gate, but remain on the road heading north for ½ mile. This brings you to the village.*

Once in the meadow go briefly down the slope, then bear right through a little area of trees and continue down to a farm track. Bear left and wander through the dry valley known as Cricketing Bottom for a little over ½ mile. About 100 yards before the track reaches a group of farm buildings the Way turns sharply to the right.

Note: *The continuing track leads to **Telscombe** for youth hostel accommodation. Go between the farm buildings and continue southwest for ½ mile or so. The track then swings left through a gate, and curves uphill to a narrow lane. Keep ahead along the lane and you come shortly to Telscombe. The youth hostel stands next to the church.*

After turning away from the track near the farm buildings, the South Downs Way hugs the foot of the slope, goes through a gate, then climbs **Mill Hill** to gain views of Seaford Head to the south-east. At the crown of the hill come onto a drive at the entrance to a house (Mill Hill) and cross directly ahead, thus joining the alternative route from Rodmell (Grid ref: 413054). The bridleway follows the garden boundary fence, then continues ahead with another wide view which includes Lewes off to the right.

For a little over a mile and a half the route makes a steady course over the typical farmed downland of **Front Hill** and **Iford Hill**. It is wide open country up here. Open to the breezes, open to the sun, with neither shade nor shelter. Passing through occasional gates the way then journeys along a concrete farm road cutting through prairie-like fields.

Mid-morning April sun beamed down and washed my shadow into the young spring corn. Out of that flint-cluttered field rose one lark after another, thrashing the air with their wings they sang as they soared higher and higher, intent on distracting my attention from their nests. What gifts their songs were for a solitary walker! Then over the brow of the hill ahead came three track-suited athletes chatting as they ran. (Lord knows where they found the breath to talk.) Within a matter of moments they were past me and pounding the concrete on the downhill slope to Mill Hill. I was relieved when they disappeared from sight, for this was a landscape that needed no human interruption. These Downs belonged to the birds and animals. Alone, I could absorb their strengths and their frailties, their past and present, their own personal songs and scents. Alone, one could share their secrets and be glad for the day. I was well content to be on my own.

After a long stretch of concrete the farm road veers hard left towards a large barn. Leave the road at this point and head off to the right for about 60 yards, then go through a gate into a sloping meadow. Turn left and keep to the top of the slope, soon joining a farm track where you maintain direction. It is a pleasant stretch to travel along – one of the best for many a long mile – for your attention is constantly being drawn down the flanks of the hills, rucked here and there by steep coombs, to the villages of Iford and Kingston-near-Lewes, with the substantial buildings of Swanborough Manor (dating from the 12th century) in between.

When the track cuts sharply to the left (where the bridleway of Breach Road crosses), continue ahead and go through a bridle gate onto a broad grassland hilltop. There is little sign of a track here, but you maintain direction and pass to the left of Kingston Hill dew pond, surrounded by gorse (Grid ref: 383078). Before long come to a second dew pond, also marked by gorse bushes, but this one lies just left of the way. It was here that Ashcombe Windmill used to spin its six sweeps (or sails) to the wind. You are now on the line of Juggs Road,[1] although there's little to show for it on the ground.

Pass through the gate and head south-westward keeping parallel with the right-hand fence, beyond which the scarp slope dips towards the busy A27 a mile and a world away. Contrast that with the cowslips at your feet and the song of larks high above! Near the end of this long meadow veer leftwards to find another bridle gate. Through this turn half-right and follow another fence. The South Downs Way now slopes downhill on the western side of Cold Coombes, soon gaining a clear view across this fine rich downland. The way passes alongside the beechwood of Newmarket Plantation, then passing through two or three more gates, leads beneath a railway arch, emerging near the A27. (The former route used to cross just to the east of this point near the Newmarket Inn.) Now the Way turns hard left between fences and comes to a private road. Go up this and across the A27 on a bridge, then bear right to pass alongside the grey, square building of **Housedean Farm** (Grid ref: 369092).

Note: *Should you be in need of accommodation, continue beyond the farm alongside the road to where a bus stop has a frequent service to **Lewes**. (Tourist Information Centre: 187 High Street, Lewes BN7 2DE ☎ 01273 483448.)*

Items of Interest:

1: Juggs Road is a one-time trading route across the South Downs used by fisher-folk from Brighton. 'Juggs' was the name given to these traders by the people of Lewes, supposedly from the earthenware jugs, or pots, in which the fish were salted and kept fresh. These traders regularly carted their fish by donkey along this route to market in the county town.

SECTION 4: HOUSEDEAN (A27)
TO PYECOMBE

Distance:	**8½ miles (13½km)**
Maps:	**Harveys South Downs Way 1:40,000**
	OS Landranger 198 Brighton & The Downs 1:50,000
	OS Explorer 122 South Downs Way, Steyning to Newhaven 1:25,000
Accommodation:	**Plumpton (+ 1 mile), Ditchling (+ 1–1½ miles), Clayton, Pyecombe, Patcham Youth Hostel (+ 2½ miles)**
Refreshments:	**None on the route until Pyecombe**

Between the heavy traffic of the A27 outside Lewes and the A23 at Pyecombe, the South Downs provide an oasis of calm, and reward with birdsong and the bleating of sheep. Much of this stretch of the Downs has been put to the plough, arable replacing pasture, but around Ditchling Beacon the downland is protected as a Nature Reserve, and it remains much as it would have been for centuries. Wide views become commonplace, but earlier, in a 'back-country' of folded hills blocked by woodland crowns, you lose all sense of height and spaciousness as the route leads between large fields with no plunging scarp slope to draw perspective.

It is another historic area with a number of ancient sites along the way. During the first part, beyond Balmer Down, the track passes west of flower-rich Mount Harry where, in 1264, Simon de Montfort took arms against Henry III in the Battle of Lewes, the outcome of which led to our present Parliamentary system. On Plumpton Plain is the site of a Bronze Age settlement. In Ditchling village below the Downs, the Romans had a fortified camp.

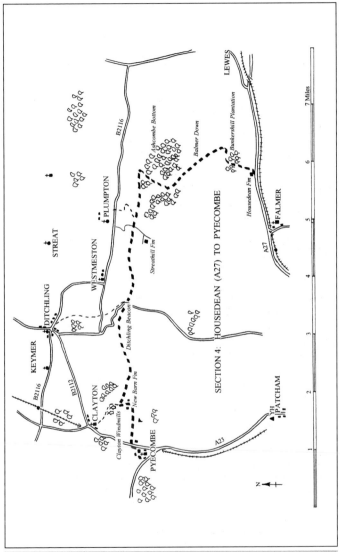

SECTION 4: HOUSEDEAN (A27) TO PYECOMBE

(Stretches of Roman road may still be detected traversing west-east at the foot of the Downs.)

The initial part of the route from Housedean Farm and the A27 replaces the former trail which led through Ashcombe Plantation. Now the way climbs Long Hill, goes through Bunkershill Plantation and rejoins the 'old' route in the arable fields of Balmer Down. The Downs of sheep-grazed grassland are to be found on Plumpton Plain with the trail heading west to Ditchling Beacon, where the South Downs Way reaches its highest point in Sussex, but where solitude is rare. Less than two miles later a pair of windmills rise out of the fields ahead – Jack and Jill, the well-known Clayton Windmills. Skirting these to the south, a track slopes downhill beside a golf course and comes to the main road a short distance from Pyecombe.

Heading east alongside the flint wall which surrounds **Housedean Farm**, turn left when the wall ends, ascend some steps and, going through a gate, continue up a sloping field to Long Hill. The head of the slope coincides with the top of the field, and in the left-hand corner another gate gives access to the woodland shown on the map as **Bunkershill Plantation**. The bridleway soon begins to descend quite steeply, and on emerging from the woods, it swings to the right between fences. At the end of this fence-enclosed section come to a crossing path and turn left.

There follows a lengthy stretch as you rise gently along the arable slopes of **Balmer Down** for a mile or so, passing a dew pond on the right and, later, going beneath a line of power cables you come to a crossing track and bear right. This bridlepath leads away from arable land, takes you between hedges and alongside a small woodland before coming to a farm track where you turn left (Grid ref: 370125). To the right of this turning is the National Trust downland of Blackcap.

Very soon you come to the scarp edge along Plumpton Plain, with a Wealden panorama to enjoy stretching far to the north. The village of Plumpton is clearly seen below with the extensive buildings of its agricultural college, the glimmer of a lake at 16th century Plumpton Place and, further north, the outline of Plumpton Racecourse.

Note: *A little under a mile after turning along Plumpton Plain is a track heading off to the right which descends to **Plumpton**, and is the one to take if you plan to stay there overnight.*

A short distance beyond the Plumpton track mentioned above, cross a narrow road leading to Streathill Farm and continue ahead, but the way eventually curves a little to the left over Western Brow, then veers right along Home Brow towards another narrow road and car park at **Ditchling Beacon**.[1] As you come to this road there is a dew pond on the left (Grid ref: 334129).

Note: *For accommodation in **Ditchling** bear right and walk down the road for about 50 yards to find a path which soon plunges down the slope among trees. At the foot of the slope maintain direction to Underhill Lane. Bear left, and 100 yards later turn right into Nye Lane. When this forks take the left-hand option leading to the village.*

Go through the car park (there is usually an ice cream van here in summer) and keep ahead, passing a little to the right of the trig point (813ft/248m). The way leads through a Nature Reserve, passes another dew pond and, little more than a mile from Ditchling Beacon, edges past a tall wooden signpost known as the Keymer Post which marks the boundary between East and West Sussex. Just beyond this the first sighting of the **Clayton Windmills**[2] is made, rising out of the fields ahead. Shortly before the windmills you come to a crossing track and turn left.

Note: *To find accommodation in **Clayton** do not turn left, but go ahead on the track, then take a path on the right which leads round the side of the first windmill (Jack). This continues past the second mill (Jill) and descends to Underhill Lane, Clayton.*

The track leads between buildings at **New Barn Farm**, and 100 yards later, at crosstracks, you turn right on an enclosed bridleway alongside a golf course. Sloping downhill eventually pass to the right of the clubhouse and come to the A273 Haywards Heath to Brighton road. Cross with care, and bear left on a narrow bush-enclosed path leading into **Pyecombe** (*accommodation, refreshments*). Turn right into School Lane and soon reach the parish church (Grid ref: 292126).

Note: *If you plan to spend the night at **Patcham Youth Hostel**, turn left by the church and walk down Church Lane which leads to a* *garage next to The Plough Inn. The bus stop for Brighton is by the garage.*

Pyecombe is a small village wedged between the A273 and A23. Its flint and pebbledash Norman church has a squat 13th century tower and, inside, a large lead font. The tapsell, or pintle, gate which leads into the churchyard has a shepherd's crook as its latch – the village is famed for the manufacture of these crooks which were used by shepherds throughout the South Downs. In 1603 the original village was hit by plague.

Items of Interest:

1: Ditchling Beacon, the highest of the South Downs in Sussex, is owned by the National Trust, with a nature reserve in the care of the Sussex Wildlife Trust. The summit is surrounded by the rectangular outline of an Iron Age hill fort.

2: The Clayton Windmills (Jack and Jill) are a much-loved feature of the South Downs. Jack, the upper, black-painted smock mill built in 1866, has been converted to a private residence and was once the home of Henry Longhurst, the golfer, but Jill, the gleaming white post mill, is in the care of a preservation society and is open to the public most weekends between May and September. Built in 1821, Jill originally stood in Patcham, Brighton, but was towed by oxen to her present site, where she worked until 1909.

SECTION 5: PYECOMBE TO BOTOLPHS
(Adur Valley)

Distance:	7½ miles (12km)
Maps:	Harveys South Downs Way 1:40,000
	OS Landranger 198 Brighton & The Downs 1:50,000
	OS Explorer 122 South Downs Way, Steyning to Newhaven 1:50,000
Accommodation:	Poynings, Truleigh Hill Youth Hostel, Bramber (+ 1½ miles), Steyning (+ ½–1½ miles)
Refreshments:	None on the route, other than drinking water supplies at Saddlescombe and Botolphs, but via a short diversion to the Devil's Dyke Hotel

This part of the route is broken into two distinct stages. The first short leg climbs out of Pyecombe to cross West Hill, then descends to a farm and cottages at Saddlescombe which is, in true geographical terms, set as a saddle, or pass, in a coombe. Ahead rises the scrub and tree-covered Devil's Dyke, where the second stage of the route returns to the back of the Downs once more. West of Devil's Dyke the way leads across the Fulking escarpment on a regular rise and fall of hills, often with distant views blinkered by higher ground to the north. Over the cluttered summit of Truleigh Hill the track carries the South Downs Way down to the Shoreham road, then over the River Adur to meet the end of the Downs Link path near St Botolph's church.

From Pyecombe church walk ahead along Church Hill (not Church Lane), soon sloping downhill to a slip road where you bear left to cross the A23 by roadbridge. Turn left and, almost opposite *The Plough Inn*, bear right. Just beyond Hobbs Cottage go uphill on a chalk track, passing through a bridle gate. Halfway up the slope go through another gate where a sign announces Newtimber Hill, owned by the National Trust. Maintain direction to the top of the hill, then veer right alongside a fence. From here you can see the tall buildings of Brighton to the south and, back the way you have come, the Clayton Windmills. As you progress and go through yet another gate, so the Devil's Dyke shows itself clearly ahead, with the tall radio masts of Truleigh Hill beyond that.

The trail now plunges down a steep grass slope, at the foot of which you go through a bridle gate and continue down an enclosed track, sunken in places, among hedges and trees. This comes to a large farm and a row of cottages at **Saddlescombe**[1] (Grid ref: 273115) There is a drinking water tap outside a building on the left. Go ahead beyond the cottages, then veer left beyond the farm and, passing more cottages, come to a minor road.

Note: *For accommodation in **Poynings** take the footpath which parallels the road to the right.*

Cross to a broad track and go through a gate at the foot of the slope to enter Summer Down. The way climbs well to the left of the dry valley of **Devil's Dyke**,[2] curves to the right alongside railings which enclose an underground reservoir, and then forks. Take the right-hand alternative which hugs the lower edge of a sloping grass-land before easing uphill to a major crossing path. Turn right. The path winds among trees and bushes, nearly always with the red-brick *Devil's Dyke Hotel* (*refreshments*) in view. Eventually come onto the narrow lane which leads to the hotel. Cross to a gate providing access onto a broad, open downland, and head towards the radio masts of Truleigh Hill, passing well to the left of a trig point and the earthen ramparts of another Iron Age hill fort.

The way leads along Fulking escarpment, passes a Bronze Age burial barrow and then, descending Perching Hill, dips below power cables to a crossing track (Fulking to the right, Southwick to the left). The way continues ahead on an obvious chalk track sweeping between pastures on the way to **Edburton Hill** and **Truleigh Hill**. Pass alongside the large buildings and masts that are an unfortunate

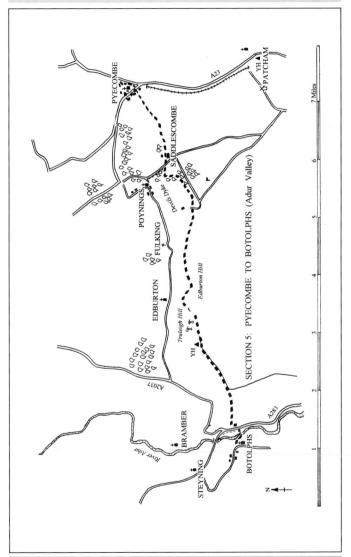

SECTION 5: PYECOMBE TO BOTOLPHS (Adur Valley)

eyesore, and maintaining direction come to **Truleigh Hill Youth Hostel** (*accommodation*) which stands beside the track to the right (Grid ref: 221107).

Continue beyond the hostel, and you will soon find a narrow footpath running parallel with the track/lane along its right-hand side. Now you should be able to see the clump of trees of Chanctonbury Ring on the edge of the downland scarp about 5 miles (8km) to the west. When the lane makes a sharp left-hand bend, go ahead through a bridle gate to follow a meadowland path which leads to a second gate. Through this an enclosed bridleway descends to the A283 Shoreham road about half a mile south of Upper Beeding (Grid ref: 197096).

Note: *From here buses serve Shoreham and Brighton in one direction, and* **Steyning** *(for accommodation and at* **Bramber**, *1½ miles) in the other.*

Bear left along the road for nearly 150 yards, then cross with care to a lay-by and an enclosed path. In a few paces come to a water tap, trough, a few seats and a sign indicating 7 miles to Washington. The way now crosses a footbridge over the River Adur, then bears right alongside the river. About 150 yards further on it swings left beside a ditch, and crosses the line of a former railway along which the Downs Link[3] has been routed. Continue ahead and come to a minor road (Grid ref: 194093) which leads to **Botolphs**. St Botolph's church stands a short distance to the left.

Botolphs is a peaceful little hamlet with neither pub nor shop, and the nearest accommodation for South Downs Way walkers being either in Bramber or Steyning. The Saxon church here glows orange towards sunset, but apart from that there is just a farm or two and a few cottages, although the village was once considerably larger and had a salt industry, and fishing. But the sea withdrew from the valley of the Adur and left Botolphs literally high and dry. In the Middle Ages its fortunes drifted out with the tide, and the odd hummocks seen in some of the meadows are all that remain of one-time village houses.

Items of Interest:

1: Saddlescombe, near the Devil's Dyke, has been farmed since before the 13th century, when it came into the ownership of the Knights Templar. In 1995 Saddlescombe Farm was acquired by the National Trust. In addition to 500 acres of agricultural land, it has several unspoiled Sussex farm buildings which include a blacksmith's forge complete with furnace and bellows.

2: The Devil's Dyke covers 183 acres of downland, but the name refers to the steep dry valley – the largest single coombe of chalk karst in Britain – cut into it. According to local legend the Devil attempted to carve a dyke through the Downs to enable the sea to flood the churches of the Weald. Working at night he shovelled the earth into great mounds, but was disturbed by an old lady carrying a candle, which he mistook for the dawn. The earth mounds are the tumuli and massive Iron Age hill fort on the summit, and the whole area is now in the care of the National Trust. Since 1987 the Trust has been running a South Downs Appeal which has seen the purchase of a number of important sites. Here in the Devil's Dyke the chalk grassland, dotted with scrub, provides a habitat for the nationally uncommon Scarce Forester moth and the Adonis Blue butterfly, while the native flora includes several orchids (among them Bee, Fragrant, Twayblade and Common Spotted), as well as wild thyme, horseshoe vetch and birdsfoot trefoil.

3: The Downs Link, as its name suggests, is a 33 mile (53km) recreational route between the North and South Downs, which follows for much of its length the bed of a dismantled railway. It begins on St Martha's Hill near Guildford, and ends at Botolphs.

SECTION 6: BOTOLPHS TO WASHINGTON

Distance:	7 miles (11km)
Maps:	Harveys South Downs Way 1:40,000
	OS Landranger 198 Brighton & The Downs 1:50,000
	OS Explorer 122 South Downs Way, Steyning to Newhaven and 121 Arundel & Pulborough 1:25,000
Accommodation:	Wiston (+ 1 mile), Washington
Refreshments:	None on the route

Climbing out of the valley of the Adur the South Downs Way soon leads onto the Downs again with lovely intimate vistas of knuckled coombs and mounded brows. A narrow country lane is crossed near the head of Steyning Bowl, then the continuing bridleway enters a broad, inner countryside of wood-lined fields over Steyning Round Hill where a number of Bronze Age cremation urns were discovered in 1949. Chanctonbury Ring is visited next. This crown of beech and sycamore, seen from so many different points along the Downs – and from the Weald below – that it has almost become a symbol of the South Downs, was badly hit by the storm of October 1987, and it will take decades before the recovery is complete.

When the South Downs Way was first opened, and it went no further west than Buriton, Chanctonbury Ring marked the halfway point. The remaining trees mark the site of an Iron Age hill fort and Roman temple, while a couple of miles or so to the south, Cissbury Ring is noted as being the largest and most impressive of earth-works on the South Downs, where remains of 200-odd Neolithic flint mines have been found. Cissbury, however, is not on the line of

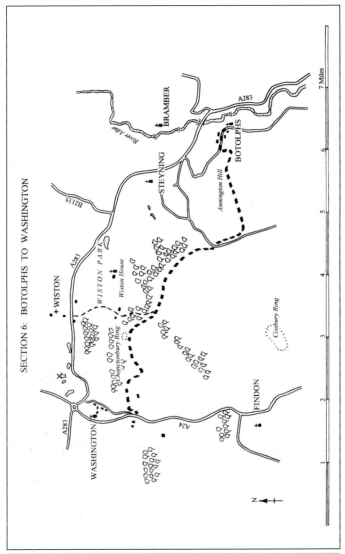

SECTION 6: BOTOLPHS TO WASHINGTON

the South Downs Way – although it would be worth visiting on a future occasion. (It is in the heart of excellent walking country.)

Once again there are no refreshments available on this stage, but for those in need of a drink or a meal when Washington is reached, a pub is found in the village.

Continue through the hamlet of **Botolphs** heading away from the church for about half a mile. The road eases uphill, curving to the right beside an attractive flint wall at Annington Old Farmhouse. Just beyond Annington House the road bends sharply to the right. Now cut off to the left along a tree-lined track which serves as the drive to a cottage. Just before reaching it the track forks. Bear right and climb on to gain the back of the Downs. As you gain height there is a tendency to keep peering off to the left where folding hills tuck themselves into Winding Bottom, a most attractive little vale with Coombe Head protecting it to the south. The sea lies not much more than three miles away, but the South Downs alignment begins to edge inland, and sea views soon recede.

The track leads to **Annington Hill** where a fairly straight route is followed heading south-west along the crest. On reaching a narrow hilltop road turn right through a gate and go along the edge of a field keeping parallel with the road. At the end of the field section exit through another gate, continue beside the road for about 200 yards, then cross left to a farm track striking through a large arable field. On coming to crosstracks note the memorial on the left, dedicated to the memory of a Sussex farmer whose ashes, along with those of his wife, were laid to rest here 'on his cherished Downs'. The left-hand track goes to Cissbury Ring and is followed by the Monarch's Way.[1] The South Downs Way continues ahead.

The way is clearly marked at all junctions, and maintains a north-westerly course among largely arable land. As you progress, so the crown of Chanctonbury Ring grows in stature ahead.

Note: *About half a mile before reaching Chanctonbury Ring, a way cuts off to the right, and descends through Chalkpit Wood by way of a track. At the foot of the Downs the track joins the narrow Chanctonbury Ring Road which leads to **Wiston**, for those who've arranged accommodation there.*

The Way continues, and rises across a green meadowland from which splendid views are to be had off to the right if you stray a little from the path. **Wiston House** is seen below, and a vast patchwork of fields, woodlands and meadows of the Weald stretching to the north, east and west. You may be able to detect the white-painted Shipley windmill (owned for many years by Hilaire Belloc), about 6½ miles away to the north. So come to **Chanctonbury Ring**[2] (Grid ref: 139120).

> *On my first walk along the South Downs Way I had looked forward to greeting the hilltop grove of beeches for some time, but feared what I might find after the ravages of the Great Storm. From afar Chanctonbury appeared to have survived. I had looked up from the depths of the Weald, and gazed at it from prominent positions along the eastern Downs and all had seemed well. But as I walked across the meadow towards it, the grey light of an overcast day shone on forlorn, leaning trunks, huge upturned discs of earth, and on the exposed and ruptured root systems. And my heart fell. For 200 years these trees had impressed themselves on the Sussex landscape, but the winds that tore across southern England in the early hours of 16 October 1987 had effectively altered the landscape. I returned several times over the ensuing years, and noted how many of the fallen trees had been removed and young trees planted in their place. Maturity will not return overnight, but nature is incredibly patient, and no doubt our children's grandchildren will be able to enjoy what we once knew as the beech crown of Chanctonbury Ring standing proud once more. Until the next major storm, that is.*

The Way skirts the Ring along its southern edge and continues heading west, but shortly after passing below a trig point, veer left-wards through a gate by a cattle grid (there is a restored dew pond on the right) and remain on the track until coming to a major junction where you turn right. Now descend a chalk and flint track which leads to a car park a little south of **Washington** (*accommodation, refreshments*) (Grid ref: 120120).

Washington village lies half a mile to the north (right) and is reached by a combination of track and road. Bypassed by the busy A24, it is a neat, compact village dating from Saxon times, with some

The parish church in Washington

attractive flint- and brick-built cottages and a parish church with 13th century columns and arches and a solid-looking 15th century tower – all that remain of the previous church which was pulled down in 1866. The pub is on the northern edge of the village, and there is a campsite beyond that, on the other side of the A283.

Items of Interest:

1: The Monarch's Way is a 609 mile (980km) long-distance walking route based on the journey taken by Charles II following defeat in the Battle of Worcester in 1651. Starting in Worcester it makes a long circuitous route and ends in Shoreham. There is a three-volume route guide written by Trevor Antill (Meridian Books).

2: Chanctonbury Ring. Planted in 1760 by Charles Goring of Wiston House, seen below to the north-east, the grove of beech and sycamore trees was especially set to please the eye. It is said that during the first few months after planting, Goring made regular visits to his young trees, carrying water up the steep slope to ensure they 'took'. An Iron Age fort of about four acres forms the base of the Ring, and following the storm of 1987 the site was properly excavated before replanting took place. The Romans had built a temple in the heart of the site during the 3rd or 4th century.

SECTION 7: WASHINGTON TO AMBERLEY

Distance:	**6 miles (9½km)**
Maps:	**Harveys South Downs Way 1:40,000**
	OS Landranger 198 Brighton & The Downs and 197 Chichester & The Downs 1:50,000
	OS Explorer 121 Arundel & Pulborough 1:25,000
Accommodation:	**Storrington (+ 1¼ miles), Amberley, Bury (+ ½ mile), Arundel Youth Hostel (+ 4½ miles, or by train + 1¼ miles)**
Refreshments:	**None on the route, other than a water tap near the start**

Between the cut made through the Downs by the valley which now carries the A24, and the twisting river valley of the Arun, the South Downs present a broad-topped escarpment, tufted here and there with trees, fields sown with wheat, barley or oil-seed rape. In places the long-distance walker or rider is rewarded with views into the depths of the Weald; sometimes over lonely farms and later, out to the glint and glimmer of the River Arun drawing itself through the low country of the north. Down there too, best seen from Rackham Banks, are the water-meadows of Amberley Wild Brooks – marshlands drained by dykes and ditches, a criss-cross of watercourses picked out by the sun. Beyond the marshes and Arun's valley the wall of the Downs slopes onward in an enticing arc.

It is another stage without habitation, although there are one or two isolated barns, and at Chantry Hill and Springhead Hill narrow lanes come onto the lip of the Downs from Storrington, whose village houses are tucked against the northern slopes. Cattle graze

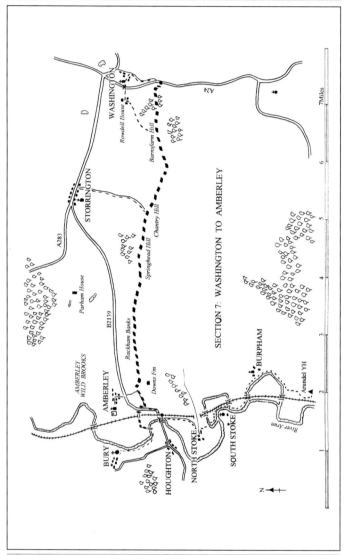

SECTION 7: WASHINGTON TO AMBERLEY

Wilmington from Wilmington Hill above the Long Man's head (Section 1a)

Paragliders, like giant butterflies, above Bostal Hill (Section 2)

Bostal Hill is a fine viewpoint from which to study the Weald (Section 2)

Telscombe Youth Hostel: accommodation in a secluded setting (Section 2)

Southease church has a rare 12th-century circular tower (Section 2)

Home Brow, to the east of Ditchling Beacon (Section 4)

Wiston Farm, below Chanctonbury Ring (Section 6)

*in large open meadows. There are hares and peewits and big skies
conjuring Turner canvases on wild-weather days.*

*Please note that the crossing of the A24 at Washington calls for
great care. Traffic travels very fast here. Should you consider it too
dangerous, an alternative to the main route is offered. See below.*

From Washington car park bear left. On the edge of the A24 a sign
indicates a safer alternative crossing, which adds about two miles to
the route. This is described below. The main South Downs Way
crosses the dual carriageway and enters Glaseby Lane. This winds
uphill and about 200 yards from the main road leads past a drinking
water supply on the left. The surfaced lane ends in a woodland, and
continues as a flint track rising up the slopes of Highden Hill. Away
to the left the large woodland of Highden Beeches contrasts the open
fields through which the track leads, and eventually you come onto
the crest of **Barnsfarm Hill** where the alternative route from
Washington joins the main South Downs Way (Grid ref: 104119).

Alternative route avoiding A24: *Turn right on the edge of A24
and follow the minor road which leads down to **Washington** village.
Bear left into The Street, and just beyond the parish church use the
bridge which crosses the A24. (Once across this a quick return to the
Way is possible by turning left on a footpath along the top of the A24
embankment, then curve south-west through woodland to rejoin the
track of the South Downs Way.) Across the A24 bridge continue
ahead as far as **Rowdell House**, then turn left (south) on a bridleway
which soon curves south-west and rises up the slopes of Barnsfarm
Hill to rejoin the South Downs Way at grid ref: 104119.*

The way continues towards a Dutch barn and, following a fence
line across the grassland of Sullington Hill, comes at last to a small
car parking area at the head of a narrow lane on **Chantry Hill** overlooking Storrington. This is a noted local viewpoint, and a place
where horses are often brought to exercise. Standing just to the right
of the SDW track is the Chantry Post, similar to the Keymer Post seen
near Ditchling Beacon on Section 4.

Note: *If you intend to seek accommodation in **Storrington** leave
the Way here and travel down the lane which leads directly to the
village.*

I had already been walking for several hours when I arrived at the Chantry Post, so sat with my back against it to eat my sandwiches. Almost immediately the heavy clouds that had been overhanging Storrington swung away to the south-west, rose up the hillside and perched sullenly on Springhead Hill to block my advance. The air turned cool, a breeze huffed across the Downs and suddenly lightning streaked the sky. Thunder roared and the ground shook. There was nowhere to hide, no shelter from the rain that came racing in great rods from the west, so I put my sandwiches away, pulled on waterproofs and headed into the eye of the storm. A magical pathway then led between shafts of lightning (fenceposts of fire), though I saw little of the countryside to the right or left, blinkered as I was by the visor of my cagoule. Twenty minutes later the worst was over and I resumed my lunch among the puddles of a dripping spinney.

With the Chantry Post to your right continue straight ahead along a clear flint track which gently crosses a line of minor hills in a north-westerly direction. In places (so I have found since that first storm-bound journey) a view opens to the left to show the sea and the outline of the Isle of Wight far off. On meeting the head of another narrow lane on **Springhead Hill**, where there is also a car park, the route veers slightly left. There are hedges and clumps of trees and much arable farmland as you approach Rackham Hill. After passing through a copse the track forks. Take the right-hand option.

All around Rackham Hill there are tumuli. To the south, a mile or so away and reached by a track known as the Lepers Way, is the site of a Bronze Age barrow (The Burgh), while ahead, alongside the route over Amberley Mount, there are lynchets which an archaeological survey revealed as a system of 20 fields, some of which had been terraced 2500 years ago.

Along the track by **Rackham Banks** you gain those splendid open views into the Weald where Parham House sprawls in its deer park backed by extensive woodland. Then ahead (west) across the Arun's gap, to the wooded slopes of the South Downs curving far into the distance luring you on. It is a lovely stretch to walk and, presumably, also to ride. Easy underfoot, easy on the eye; a peaceful, generous

South Path, the lane which runs down to Amberley

landscape. Eventually the way leads down to a gate with the large conglomeration of barns and outbuildings of **Downs Farm** seen below. Go through the gate and descend the slope to pass well to the right of the farm. An enclosed bridlepath then leads to a road where you bear right for about 80 yards. On coming to a junction where you gain a sneak view of Amberley[1] turn left into High Titten (Grid ref: 034125).

Note: *For those needing accommodation in Amberley do not turn left here but continue ahead down the lane known as South Path. This meets the B2139 at minor crossroads. Cross directly ahead into the village where there is a pub, village store and b&b.*

High Titten slopes downhill between deep chalk quarries, although that on the right is mostly hidden by bushes and trees. That on the left contains Amberley Museum[2] which can be seen between the trees, while sometimes you can hear the whistle of a steam engine deeply below. On reaching the B2139 turn right onto a raised path running alongside the road towards **Amberley**. (*Refreshments available at both pub and café 500 yards down the road to the left.*)

Note: *If your plan is to stay overnight in **Arundel Youth Hostel** (☎ 01903 882204) turn left along the B2139 and follow this down to Amberley railway station – pub and café nearby. Trains run south from here to Arundel – the next station. From Arundel station turn right alongside the busy road, then cross to the first minor road signposted to Burpham. The youth hostel is situated about a mile along it. Alternatively, just beyond Amberley station turn left along Stoke Road, and after coming to North Stoke, take a footpath south and, when reaching the river, continue along the left bank. This leads to Burpham, but you continue south of the village, cutting away from the river where it makes a right-hand curve. The path then goes almost directly to the youth hostel – a little over 4 miles from Amberley station.*

When the path beside the B2139 runs out, cross the road with care and continue on a path now on the left of the road, behind a hedge. This brings you to a concrete farm drive where you turn left, soon to cross the railway line. Beyond a water treatment plant maintain direction on a track which twists around fields and brings you to the River Arun.[3] Bear right to a bridleway bridge, provided in 1994 by the Sussex Downs Conservation Board as part of a safer alternative to the original South Downs Way route, which previously followed the busy road into Houghton.

Note: *For accommodation in **Bury** cross the bridge and turn right to follow the riverside path all the way to the village.*

Items of Interest:

1: Amberley is one of the most attractive of all Sussex villages, and is well worth a visit. It has many charming thatched cottages, and others whose gardens cascade over their walls. Next to the Norman church stand the ruins of a 14th century castle built for the Bishops of Chichester around a former manor house. North of the village stretch Amberley Wild Brooks ('Wild' is a derivation of 'Weald'), an area of some 30 acres of grazing marshes and water meadows spreading out from the Arun.

One of many attractive houses in the village of Amberley

2: Amberley Museum was created from a large chalk quarry on the east bank of the Arun, which at one time employed more than 100 men. The 36 acre site has a variety of industrial machinery on display, as well as a narrow gauge railway, blacksmith's shop, clay-pipemaker's and woodturner's shops and a printing works. The museum is open to the public between May and October, Weds-Suns, and daily during the school summer holidays.

3: The River Arun is the longest in Sussex, rising in St Leonard's Forest near Crawley and discharging into the sea at Littlehampton. It is a popular river with anglers, for whom chub, pike, perch and roach are tempted. There is a very pleasant riverside walk between Amberley and Arundel, while the bankside path continues all the way to the estuary at Littlehampton. During the Napoleonic Wars a canal was built to join the Arun with the Thames via the River Wey. A wharf stood on the river then, near Houghton bridge, and chalk barges traded along the navigation. The canal was closed in 1868.

SECTION 8: AMBERLEY TO COCKING

Distance:	12 miles (19km)
Maps:	Harveys South Downs Way 1:40,000
	OS Landranger 197 Chichester & The Downs 1:50,000
	OS Explorer 121 Arundel & Pulborough and 120 Chichester 1:25,000
Accommodation:	Gumber Bothy + Camping (+ 1 mile), Graffham (+ 1 mile) Heyshott (+ 1½ miles), Cocking (+ ¾ mile)
Refreshments:	None on the route, except water tap on the outskirts of Cocking, but pub in Houghton, 400 yards off-route near the start

Given private transport arrangements this lengthy stage could be broken either at Bignor Hill, or after about 6 miles at the crossing of A285 south of Petworth. Not long after crossing the River Arun you meet the halfway point between Eastbourne and Winchester. A signpost where the South Downs Way crosses the A29 near Coombe Wood announces 50 miles to Winchester, 51 back to Eastbourne – a notable milepost on the long journey. Between this point and Bignor Hill the way pushes through an agricultural landscape where large fields fold into neat valleys and woodlands sit on the hills. Bignor Hill conjures up the Roman era, for the South Downs Way briefly shares the route of the Roman Stane Street. Burton Down gives way to more arable farmland, but west of the A285 there is much woodland and for several miles views are severely restricted. Strips of farmland break up the extensive woods, but once Manorfarm Down is reached, vistas open once more above the little village of Cocking – a village with an attractive heart and welcome prospects of refreshment and lodging.

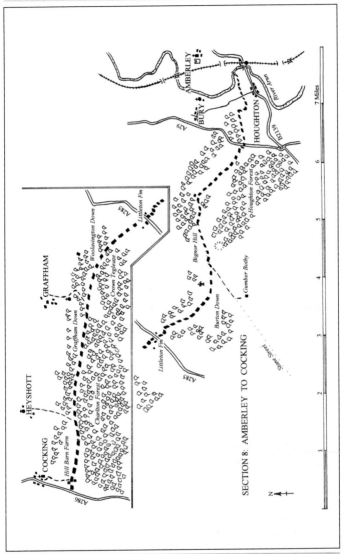

SECTION 8: AMBERLEY TO COCKING

Cross the bridleway bridge over the Arun and bear right along the west bank. When the river curves to the right, leave the embankment to cut left on a bridleway alongside a drainage ditch. On the far side of the field turn right and soon go through a gate on the left. Continue to the Houghton–Bury road. (*Refreshments in Houghton*[1] *400 yards to the left.*) Cross this minor road and maintain direction on a track sloping gently uphill. It snakes round to the right above a lovely little valley, and still rising offers views of the twisting Arun below, and the village of Bury[2] beside it. Now the track curves left and at the top of the slope brings you alongside Coombe Wood to reach the A29 (Grid ref: 004118). Bear right for 100 yards, then follow a chalk track on the left towards **Houghton Forest**. From this track look back to enjoy a wonderful panoramic view which includes the Weald, Amberley Wild Brooks, distant downland ridges, and the Arun sidling through the valley. Beside the forest the way bears right, soon leaving the edge of the trees to cut through open fields on Bury Hill. (*'To this green hill a something dreamlike clings…'* said Galsworthy in his poem *Bury Hill.*)

The track becomes enclosed by fences and bordered by cowslips among the banks of Westburton Hill. Sloping downhill the way brings you to some barns in a sunken hollow, and just beyond these there's a junction of tracks. Bear left, then immediately turn right to climb uphill alongside hedges, over cross-tracks and ahead beside a fence marking the way to **Bignor Hill**. To the north, at the foot of the Downs, lie the ruins of Bignor Roman Villa.

Shortly before gaining the summit of Bignor Hill, the way used to pass a mounting block known as Toby's Stone – a memorial to one-time secretary of the Cowdray Hounds, Toby Wentworth-Fitzwilliam – but by the spring of 1999 this had been vandalised and almost completely destroyed.

Over Bignor Hill is a car park close to the line of the Roman Stane Street,[3] and an interesting finger post bearing Latin names: *Noviomagus* (Chichester) and *Londinium* (London). Passing this post to your left continue ahead towards a pair of aerials. About 200 yards from the post bear left along the agger (or embankment) of Stane Street, then right at the first junction (Grid ref: 970128).

Note: *If you plan to spend the night at the National Trust's* **Gumber Bothy** *(a Camping Barn with 27 sleeping places, kitchen and* *showers – tents allowed nearby) do not turn right here, but continue ahead along Stane Street for ¾ mile, then veer left at a signed junction. The bothy is just 1 mile from the South Downs Way – not 1¾ miles as the Bignor Hill signpost suggests.*

Having turned right away from the route of Stane Street, in a few paces go through a gate into a field below the aerial masts, and maintain direction alongside a fence. On the far side of the field exit through another bridle gate and continue over cross-tracks. Passing a few yew trees on **Burton Down** the way heads north-west across arable land (the woods on the right descend the scarp slope into the delightfully-named Scotcher's Bottom), and then descends through woods on a clear track which brings you to the A285 Petworth–Chichester road at **Littleton Farm** (Grid ref: 951144).

> *Coming down the track in the mid-afternoon, birds were mostly silent, but there were numerous wild flowers clustered at the base of the trees and along wayside banks to brighten the walk. Small flies danced as though riding gossamer yo-yos in misted beams of sunlight that chequered the track around me. I wandered down on stepping stones of shadow.*

Cross the road and take the track opposite which passes to the right of the farm between grassy banks and trees. On coming to cross-tracks go into the field ahead (to the right of a rising track) and cross uphill through the field, veering slightly to the right in order to find another bridle gate in a mid-field fence, then continue to the upper edge of the top field.

> *My heart went into my mouth as a partridge leapt out of the young corn beside me, and when I recovered from the shock and looked around, I saw the pleading eyes of the hen bird gazing pitifully from her maternal egg-protecting squat. The cock had raced away to distract my attention, leaving the hen bravely sitting out the danger. 'Bloody daft place to lay your eggs!' I scolded, 'the path'll be crawling with ramblers 'ere long.' Leaving her in peace, I almost detected her sigh of relief.*

At the head of the field a broad track leads into woodland above Stickingspit Bottom near the high point of **Crown Tegleaze**

(830ft/253m). This is the start of a long section with no buildings in sight for more than three miles, much of the way devoid of views. It goes through and alongside woods over **Woolavington Down** and **Graffham Down**, the dense woodlands hiding deer, the seemingly endless rectangular fields between the woods haunted by pheasants. There are several alternative paths and tracks cutting from it, but the route of the South Downs Way is obvious, if not waymarked at every junction.

Note: *At the end of a long field section, where the way becomes pincered by woods once more on Graffham Down, a junction of tracks marked by an oak signpost, offers one of two ways by which to divert to **Graffham** – below the Downs to the north (right) for overnight accommodation.*

On the way through the woods on Graffham Down, note two open sites (one on the right, the other to the left of the track) where patches of downland are managed by the Graffham Down Trust to protect the chalk-loving plants and butterflies. For some time you remain enclosed by woodland, then the way opens a little and the track kinks left then right on Heyshott Down where, on the right, there is an archaeological site containing a group of Bronze Age burial mounds. In the middle of the next hedged field there is a trig point and a tall, timber-built shooting platform. Beyond this the track cuts through more woodland, then alongside yet more woods on the edge of a large open field.

It was late in the day and I'd seen no-one for several hours, but I'd not been alone as there was plenty of wildlife for company. Now I spied a dog fox padding with exaggerated stealth across the field before me, head forward, back low, tail extended. The field was being picked over by innumerable pheasants, and the fox had one unsuspecting bird in its sights. Dinner was less than a minute away when, for some unknown reason, the fox glanced in my direction. He froze – as did I. Then in-built fear spun him around and, forsaking his meal (or at least, postponing it) he raced for the cover of the woods. I sensed, rather than heard, his curses. But there were no thanks from the pheasants, which continued their scrabbling undisturbed.

The flint track then descends through more open countryside as Manorfarm Down spreads itself fanshape to the west. And at last you come to the buildings of **Hill Barn Farm** about 250 yards before the A286 on Cocking Hill. There is a drinking water tap on the left of the track by the entrance to a sawmill.

Note: *To reach* **Cocking** *for accommodation, refreshments, or to stock up with supplies from the village store, bear right through the farm on a track leading down to the village, which you reach below the charming little church. Take the lane left of the church and this will bring you to the heart of Cocking by the village store, close to the Blue Bell Inn.*

The Way continues beyond Hill Barn Farm and soon reaches the Midhurst–Chichester road (Grid ref: 875166). There is a bus stop nearby which is useful if you plan to divert from the route to visit either Midhurst to the north, or Chichester to the south. **Cocking** lies ¾ mile down the road to the right.

Cocking is a small village astride the A286, but away from the road it remains remarkably unspoiled. Several of the houses in and around the village belong to the Cowdray Estate, their window frames painted custard yellow. There was a settlement here before the Norman conquest, and the Domesday Book records '...a church, 6 serfs and 5 mills yielding 37 shillings and sixpence.' The church stands on the eastern end of the village with fields around it, and is worth visiting. Manor Farm shares the churchyard wall, and below it runs a clear stream in a peaceful setting. About 3½ miles to the south at Singleton, the Weald & Downland Open Air Museum is a fascinating collection of traditional buildings in a rural setting – well worth a visit on a future occasion.

Items of Interest:

1: Houghton stands a little above the River Arun, and the South Downs Way used to go through it until a diversion took the route away from the busy road. The village has several interesting buildings, one of which is the *George & Dragon*, where the young Charles II supposedly stopped for refreshment in October 1651 during his flight to France following defeat in the Battle of Worcester.

2: Bury is a neighbour both to Houghton and Amberley, an attractive riverside village (there used to be a ferry allowing easy access to Amberley) with a secluded air about it. Novelist John Galsworthy lived in the mock-Tudor Bury House from 1926 until his death in 1933.

3: Stane Street is a Saxon name for the Roman road built in AD 70 for both military and economic purposes to link Chichester (*Noviomagus*) with London (*Londinium*). It was metalled and had a camber, and was 20–25 feet (6–7½m) wide. This remarkable piece of engineering had to cross not only the South and North Downs, but also the greensand range of hills and the almost impenetrable Wealden forest. It achieved the 56 mile (90km) route in three straight lines, including a passage through the 2000 acre estate attached to the Roman Villa at Bignor. This is found below the Downs a short distance away from the point at which the South Downs Way crosses. Bignor Roman Villa is open to the public throughout the year, with the exception of Mondays between October and March.

SECTION 9: COCKING TO SOUTH HARTING

Distance:	**7½ miles (12km)**
Maps:	**Harveys South Downs Way 1:40,000**
	OS Landranger 197 Chichester & The Downs 1:50,000
	OS Explorer 120 Chichester 1:25,000
Accommodation:	**Elsted (+ 1 mile), South Harting (+ ¾ mile)**
Refreshments:	**None on the route**

This stage of the South Downs Way makes a very fine journey, full of variety and interest. There are sections where the views are extensive, and others in which woodland draws a secluded landscape. There are isolated farms tucked away from the world just off the trail, with practically no other habitation and no villages of any size for many a long mile. Once again the route hugs the northern edge of the escarpment, but gazing south it is possible to catch a glimpse of Chichester's cathedral spire framed within a tree-crowded panorama. In the woods encroaching on the trail you may catch sight of deer. Certainly there will be numerous birds to serenade the day, and wild flowers in plenty.

An easy track leads onto Cocking Down, then to Linch Down, broad and open. Monkton Down leads to Philliswood, and emerging from the light glades of these woodlands a delightful countryside is revealed. On the approach to Beacon Hill one rejoices in the landscape, and over Harting Down the northern slopes plunge to tiny communities snug in the shadow of the Downs. Rarely will you travel this last downland brow alone, for there is a car park nearby and a road that leads from Petersfield. Across this the SDW bridleway continues to a second road, the

B2146, which has a path running adjacent to it down to South Harting, while the main route avoids the village and aims towards Hampshire. But this is reserved for Section 10.

Yet again this stage is entirely without refreshment (except by diversion from the route), so set out for the day suitably provisioned.

From the A286 south of Cocking village the South Downs Way heads north-west along Middlefield Lane, passing a farm and rising towards Cocking Down. The white chalk track is enclosed by hedges at first, but on gaining the crest of the Downs bare fences replace them. Off to the left stretches an extensive area of woodland, inhabited by deer, some of which emerge at night in small herds to sleep in the wheat-fields, thus flattening the crops and causing problems at harvest time.

For three miles the track maintains a steady north-westerly direction across Cocking Down, Linch Down (with the trig point of Linch Ball in the middle of a field to the right), and Didling Hill. On the proverbial clear day, not only Chichester Cathedral may be seen across the intervening woods, but also the Solent and the Isle of Wight beyond that. This crown of hills has mostly been turned to arable farmland, but there is grassland on Didling Hill white with sheep, grazing fenced meadows that need no shepherd to keep watch. Then the track is absorbed into a tunnel of trees and scrub, with a high fence on the left containing the secluded, virtually unseen, **Monkton House**. In its grounds peacocks can be heard screeching.

One peacock had somehow escaped the lofty barrier and ran ahead of me along the muddy track, its exotic feathers dragging behind, reminding me of a bride opting for extravagant fashion in place of traditional white. Now and then it stopped to check if I were still following, then took off once more. Stupid bird, I feared I might chase it all the way to Winchester.

The track swings to the left with open meadows on the right, and by a stile a small memorial stone bears the simple inscription: 'Mark liked it here. 23.7.60–20.4.98.' Just ahead, on the edge of Philliswood, a series of curious mounds can be seen – the tumuli, or burial mounds, known as the Devil's Jumps, which date from the Bronze Age – about 3500 years ago. **Philliswood Down** is clothed in

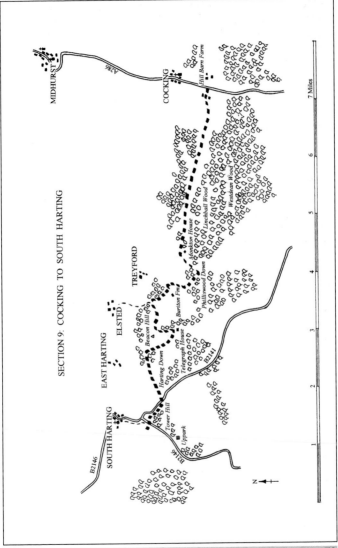

SECTION 9: COCKING TO SOUTH HARTING

lovely mature beech, oak and birch trees, and the Way takes you through the woodland into a delight of birdsong in the morning, among multi-shades of green in the leaves, on the trunks and in the ground cover of sunlit glades.

Come to a crossing track and break away sharply to the right. As the way slopes downhill it joins a broader track, eventually leaving the woods behind to gain views ahead which include the little communities of Treyford and Elstead in the distance. Across to the left the shape of Telegraph House[1] can sometimes be seen above the trees on the southern slope of Beacon Hill.

Coming to a narrow farm track (Grid ref: 821178), with **Buriton Farm** huddled in a dip of folding hills to the left, bear left for a few paces, then turn right (there are no waymarks) through a bridle gate onto an enclosed track heading north-west once more. The way skirts the edge of a spinney , then along the bottom edge of a field to a crossing track (Grid ref: 816184).

Note: *If you have planned to spend the night at **Elsted**, bear right here. The village is about 1 mile away to the north.*

Cross straight ahead, then veer left to climb the slope along a scrub-and-thorn margin between fields. This is Pen Hill, and from the crest there is a splendid panorama to enjoy.

On my most recent journey along this route rain cascaded down and created a fine mist through which no views could be seen at all. But I recalled my first wandering here, which offered a total contrast: I'd stripped off my shirt in the spring warmth, and lay for a while in the grass gazing into a hazy blue vault where half a dozen skylarks trilled with an enthusiasm impossible to check. Turning to the east my eye caught the sweeping Downs brunched with spring colours in the trees and shrubs of the northern slopes. To the west Beacon Hill, site of an Iron Age hill fort of forty acres, was scarred with two distinct white tracks across which shadowy four-legged figures loped to and fro. Far views were distorted, but that did not matter. Nearer to hand there were flowers in the field margins and blossom among the blackthorn. I saw a rabbit break cover and nervously make a stuttering run across the bay below. Ants pioneered a new route up the face of an upturned

Amberley is one of the most attractive Sussex villages (Section 7)

The Way as it passes between Westburton Hill and Bignor Hill (Section 8)

The River Meon, a lovely chalk stream, at Exton (Section 11)

slice of flint. A pheasant cackled, a cuckoo called, while sheep in valley meadows sent messages in the breeze. Unused to such busy peace, city folk might call it silence. It was not. In the calm hush of morning were countless sounds of life – but nothing at all with an engine. All was just as it should have been. There was undisturbed perfection in the slow revolving minutes, as I lay there and absorbed it all in solitude.

Before leaving Pen Hill, study Beacon Hill to the west and note that it is the left-hand chalk track that should be taken (although the right-hand option makes a short cut over the summit of the hill and rejoins the South Downs Way proper at Bramshott Bottom, thus saving about ¾ mile). Descend steeply into the saddle between Pen Hill and **Beacon Hill**, then fork left to traverse round the east slope above the coomb known as Millpond Bottom. The way takes you along the edge of a large field and comes to trees, scrub and gorse bushes near the entrance to **Telegraph House**. At a crossing track by the entrance, head sharply to the right along a scrub-lined track with a rich variety of plants growing beside it. This leads along the neat vale of Bramshott Bottom, and comes to cross-tracks in an open grassy saddle marked by a prominent wooden post set on a stone base (Grid ref: 803186). Turn left to gain **Harting Down** – a nature reserve owned by the National Trust, which is a popular excursion for motorists who park on the western side.

Do not stray to the actual summit of Harting Down, but keep along the right-hand slope where views from the springy turf are considerable. A number of small villages may be seen below, pre-eminent being South Harting with a green copper broach spire to its church. (There is also East Harting and West Harting, but whatever happened to North Harting?)

To the west of Harting Down you come to a car park, and just beyond this cross the B2141 and continue along a track which parallels the road among some fine mature beech, oak and chestnut trees. This pleasant stretch is known as The Bosom, and it cuts round the flank of **Tower Hill** to meet the B2146 above **South Harting** (*accommodation, refreshments*) (Grid ref: 783185). The village is off to the right, while to the left the road leads to Uppark and, eventually, to the coast.

Note: *If it is your intention to stay overnight in* **South Harting** *– or need refreshment at the White Hart – do not use the road, but cross on the continuing Way, then turn right on a footpath which descends through woods and enters the village just south of the church, a distance of a little over ½ mile.*

South Harting is a compact little village with a 14th century church dedicated to St Mary and St Gabriel. Shortly before he died, the Victorian novelist Anthony Trollope lived here. The village is perhaps best known for the dignified mansion of Uppark which stands on Tower Hill to the south, at which the mother of H.G. Wells was housekeeper in the late 19th century. Uppark is in the care of the National Trust; it suffered a disastrous fire in 1989, but has since been rebuilt at great expense.

Items of Interest:

1: Telegraph House is partially hidden at the end of a long drive on the south slope of Beacon Hill, and was built by Earl Russell on the site of one of the Admiralty's Portsmouth to London telegraph stations established during the Napoleonic Wars. Earl Russell's brother, the philosopher Bertrand Russell, later turned the house into a (short-lived) school.

SECTION 10: SOUTH HARTING
TO BURITON
(Queen Elizabeth Forest)

Distance:	3½ miles (5½km)
Maps:	Harveys South Downs Way 1:40,000
	OS Landranger 197 Chichester & The
	Downs 1:50,000
	OS Explorer 120 Chichester 1:25,000
Accommodation:	Buriton (+ ¼–1½ miles)
Refreshments:	None on the route

This short stage which leads to the outskirts of Buriton takes the route out of Sussex and into Hampshire, and marks the original completion of the South Downs Way before the extension to Winchester was approved in 1989. It is a stage in which there is a change in landscape, for gone – albeit temporarily – are the rolling Downs, and in their place a typically southern countryside of low farmland with woods and hedgerows and winding lanes. But it is no less interesting for that. There are plenty of spring and summer flowers in the hedgerows and field margins, and no shortage of wildlife. There will be jackdaws, no doubt, circling above the woods, and rabbits nose-twitching along the track. Peewits swoop over low-lying fields, and kestrels hover, head down, in search of an unsuspecting meal.

From the point where the previous section paused above South Harting, a two-mile hedge-lined track strikes across farmland with long views into the Weald, and reaches a farm on the Sussex– Hampshire border. A quiet country lane then takes over, before returning to a trackway at Coulters Dean Farm. At the western end

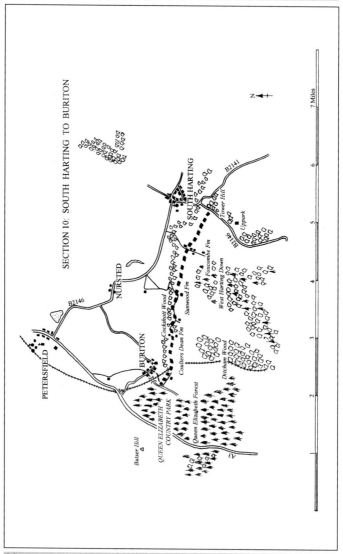

SECTION 10: SOUTH HARTING TO BURITON

of this another lane continues the route among woods on the way to Queen Elizabeth Forest, which is reached just above Buriton. Although there are no refreshment facilities along the route, Buriton (½ mile distant) has a pub which serves food.

From the B2146 above South Harting follow the clear hedge-lined track north-westward with views into the Weald to the right. The track is known as Forty Acre Lane and it leads for nearly a mile alongside gentle farmland to a narrow metalled road, which it crosses. Maintain direction on the second half of Forty Acre Lane, near the end of which, just before reaching Sunwood Farm, you leave West Sussex behind and enter Hampshire. At **Sunwood Farm** come onto a quiet country road and turn left. In a few paces the road swings to the right and eases up a gentle slope beside a row of copper beech trees.

On coming to a minor junction branch right. The road then winds through **Cockshott Woo**d, losing height among the trees. Do not be tempted by a track marked to Buriton, but remain on the road, passing Coulters Dean Nature Reserve[1] on the left shortly before reaching **Coulters Dean Farm**, which shelters in a lonely hollow. The surfaced lane ends here, but the way continues beyond the farm, now rising uphill and passing beneath overhead power cables to gain more Wealden views to the north, before coming down to Dean Barn and a pair of cottages. After these follow the metalled lane through Appleton's Copse and on to a T-junction (Grid ref: 734198) opposite a parking area with Queen Elizabeth Forest stretching ahead.

Note: *For those in need of accommodation or refreshment in **Buriton**, do not walk down the road, but take the bridleway which cuts off to the right just before reaching the T-junction. This slopes down through woods and joins South Lane under a railway bridge. Buriton lies just beyond.*

Buriton (*accommodation, refreshments*) is an unspoilt village with a large rectangular duckpond, a huddle of cottages and an Elizabethan manor house behind the parish church where the historian, Edward Gibbon (1737–94) spent his early years. The village is on a bus route to Petersfield, about three miles to the north.

Items of Interest:

1: Coulters Dean Nature Reserve is owned by the Hampshire Wildlife Trust, and is a noted habitat for 11 types of orchid. Deer and badger feed there, and a number of butterflies gather on bright summer days, among them the Adonis Blue, Chalk Hill and Holly Blue.

SECTION 11: BURITON TO EXTON

Distance:	12½ miles (20km)
Maps:	Harveys South Downs Way 1:40,000
	OS Landranger 197 Chichester & The Downs and 185 Winchester & Basingstoke 1:50,000
	OS Explorer 120 Chichester and 119 Meon Valley 1:25,000
Accommodation:	Coombe Cross, East Meon (+ 1¼ miles), West Meon (+ 1½ miles), Warnford (+ 1¼ miles), Corhampton (+ ½–2 miles)
Refreshments:	Queen Elizabeth Country Park Centre, Butser Hill, and Exton.

The first point to make about this, and the last, section of the South Downs Way, is that waymarking is not always clear, and that the map and guidebook should be consulted perhaps more often than has been the case thus far. That being said, there should be no real problems of route-finding if care be taken, while a return to true downland will be welcomed after the dense woodland cover of Queen Elizabeth Forest has been left behind.

On this section of the South Downs Way there are grassy paths, broad tracks and country lanes to follow. There are stretches of dark forest with the chance of sighting deer, open hilltops with memorable, far-reaching views, tree-and-scrub-lined trackways, big fields and rolling meadows. There is fast-moving traffic on the A3 (avoided by a subway), and an ancient site to wander through on Old Winchester Hill (walkers only here – the bridleway takes an alternative route). Butser Hill is the highest point, not just of

Hampshire but of all the South Downs, and this is crossed in the early stages after ducking beneath the A3. HMS Mercury is visited – an incongruous name to be found so far inland with neither ship nor sea in sight – and after crossing Old Winchester Hill, the Way follows a delightful and rare chalk stream to the banks of the River Meon.

For those with private transport, it would be possible to arrange to break the route at the road junction of Hyden Cross near HMS Mercury.

Go through the car park and into **Queen Elizabeth Forest** – part of the Queen Elizabeth Country Park[1] – on a broad track which curves left as it rises along the east flank of hillside where one or two simple seats enjoy views down to Buriton. Over the brow of the hill ignore the first track cutting back to the right and proceed ahead until the main track forks. At this point the footpath and bridleway routes separate: the bridleway route is the left-hand track, the footpath (walker's) route takes the right branch. (The two converge later near the Country Park Visitor Centre.) On the way through the forest keep alert for possible sightings of deer. The footpath route passes a picnic and barbecue area in Gravelhill Bottom, and eventually comes to a small car park at Benhams Bushes.

All was peaceful along the forest track, and as it was midweek it seemed that I had the forest to myself. Few birds sang, except far off, and my boots made little sound, and as I walked my eyes and ears were alert for wildlife. Suddenly I became aware of eyes upon me, and turning to the right-hand slope, saw a pair of deer gazing in my direction. No body markings could be seen, only heads to one side of a tree, rumps to the other. They watched me and I watched them, but their interest was less intense than mine – once they'd established I offered no threat – and growing bored with the view they vanished soundlessly into the deep security of the forest.

At Benhams Bushes come onto a narrow metalled road where you turn left to leave the forest (there is a path running parallel with the road on its left). As you exit the forest there are various small grassy areas and a number of laid-out paths. There is also a confusing super-

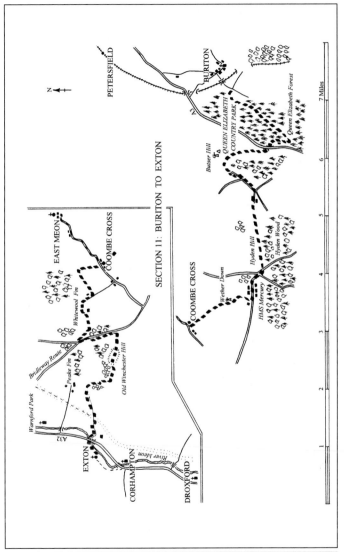

SECTION 11: BURITON TO EXTON

abundance of waymarks and signs for a variety of walks and rides, which makes it necessary to study the way well. Veer right towards the Park Visitor Centre (*refreshments, public toilets etc*). The bridleway avoids the Centre itself by remaining just within the forest, but the walker's route goes right to it.

Note: *There is a drinking water tap by the path. The Visitor Centre and Coach House Café are open daily from Easter to October (10am-5pm), and weekends from November to March (10am-dusk).*

Continue beyond the Visitor Centre on a path above and to the right of the car park. This leads under the A3 by a subway, on the west side of which you follow blue bridleway posts bearing the SDW white acorn symbol, leading across another car park/picnic area, then through a bridle gate into an extensive grassland. Ahead rises 888ft/271m **Butser Hill**[2] topped by a huge telecommunications mast. Mount the steep slope of flower-starred downland, making more or less towards the mast (there is a vague path). Near the head of the slope pause for a moment to enjoy a huge panoramic view, then go through a gate and veer left to another bridle gate near the entrance to a car park.

Note: *For refreshments bear right through the car park to a café/toilets/information centre in a building shaped like an Iron Age roundhouse.*

Bear left to Limekiln Lane which has a bridleway on its right-hand side, but which soon crosses to the left. When this eventually gives out, continue along the lane with exceptional views to enjoy, including the sea far off to the south, and the great expanse of Queen Elizabeth Forest with its straight lines of firebreaks to the west. When the lane makes a left-hand bend at a multi-way junction, take the right-hand option. Passing Homelands Farm the surfaced lane becomes a track (a true green lane), goes beneath a line of power cables and continues on an almost straight and level course across Tegdown Hill and **Hyden Hill**, alongside the oaks and beeches of **Hyden Wood** – a lovely section of ridge crest from which East Meon church can be seen off to the north-west where meadows fold neatly into a shallow valley.

Soft green shadows dappled the path. Newly-unfurled beech

*leaves were silken to the touch, and with the afternoon light
shining through them it was possible to detect the outline fuzz of
minute hairs and the rich tracery of veins within. Softly they
danced up and down in the two o'clock gasp of air so that the
route ahead was seen as through an ever-opening and closing
Venetian blind of shadow. The next time I wandered this track I
took advantage of a stile for use as a seat, and spent twenty
minutes day-dreaming across a meadow clotted with ewes and
their lambs. Within moments they all came marching towards
me from three different directions, their massed bleating
announcing their expectation of something I hadn't got. It didn't
take them long to realise I was no shepherd, and they turned
away with barely a glance behind them. If they were disap-
pointed they didn't show it, but resumed their grazing and left
me in peace.*

The track leads to a junction of minor roads at Hyden Cross (Grid ref:
683189). The road north goes to East Meon,[3] south to Clanfield and
Horndean, while we maintain direction and soon come to a second
junction near what used to be the main entrance to **HMS Mercury**.
Continue along the road veering right, and before long you pass
between Naval buildings. At the western end of the inshore establishment, just before coming to a sports field where the road veers
left and a tarred road cuts off to the right, bear right (the sports field
now on your left and the masts of **Wether Down** directly ahead) and
you find that the road soon becomes a track. This takes you directly
past the radio masts and, on Salt Hill, the site of a long barrow in the
left-hand field.

It is good to be away from buildings and a hard-surfaced road,
and on the Downs once more. Views open to the north, and although
the track is confined by a fence and hedges, there is the welcome
return to a sense of space. But then as you begin to slope downhill
the way becomes a sunken track on the approach to **Coombe Cross**
(*accommodation*). This is little more than a couple of cottages and a
Georgian house on a quiet country lane (Grid ref: 666210).

Note: *For accommodation and refreshments in **East Meon**, turn
right and walk down the lane for about 1¼ miles.*

The South Downs Way crosses the lane and continues straight

The view stretches towards Hayling Island from the crown of Butser Hill

ahead towards the rise of Henwood Down, but about ½ mile from the road, at a crossing bridleway, turn left on a track which leads along the right-hand side of a large field and eventually comes onto a concrete farm road which you follow to its end at a minor road.

A big open country spreads before you. Fields are gold with oil-seed rape, green or yellow with corn, soft with meadows grazed by black and white Friesian cows. The Downs are rolled out as if for inspection. Henwood Down stands again to the north, the wooded rise of Old Winchester Hill is off to the west, and knowing our route leads across it, it seems odd that you now head away to the north. But those who would walk from A to B by the shortest route should have been with Caesar's troops and forget all about modern long-distance footpaths!

Turn right, passing Hall Cottages, then break away to the left at the entrance to **Whitewool Farm**. Go down the farm drive between small lakes and skirt the handsome half-thatched outbuildings, then bear right on another concrete farm road that soon deteriorates to a rutted track. At a junction of tracks veer right and ascend the slopes of Whitewool Hanger, at the top of which the track emerges at a junction of narrow lanes (Grid ref: 645217).

Note: *At this point the route for cyclists and horse riders leaves that of the walker. The 'bridleway' route (apparently only a temporary arrangement) is waymarked to the north-west along Old Winchester Hill Lane to* **Warnford** *(accommodation, refreshments) in the Meon Valley, and beyond to Wheely Down Farm where the way reverts to a track along the route of the Monarch's Way once more, to rejoin the walker's SDW at* **Beaconhill Beeches** *(Grid ref: 59827). An alternative route has been proposed – but has yet to be accepted – which would lead the bridleway south of Old Winchester Hill and rejoin the walker's route near Exton. Watch for notices and waymarks.*

Walkers should turn left along the road for about 400 yards to find a car park for **Old Winchester Hill** on the right. Just inside this a gate on the left gives access to a path which runs parallel with the road, and eventually (after a further 500 yards or so) comes to a crossing flint track which carries the official South Downs Way from a layby for disabled people (the so-called 'Easygoing Trail' car park). The flint track is the Easygoing Trail, a level path created to give access for the less able-bodied to Old Winchester Hill fort.[4] Turn right along this trail and follow it to the hill fort entrance. Go through the gate and veer left, then take the path which cuts through the centre of this impressive Iron Age site. There are big views to enjoy too, with a distant sighting of Chichester Harbour, and the Isle of Wight out to the south-west.

On coming to the earth ramparts on the western side of the fort go down the steep slope half-left (yellow with cowslips in spring) to leave the fort area, then along a fence-enclosed path beside a wood. Beyond the wood the path is directed to the right round the edge of fields (the OS Explorer map suggests an alternative route, but at the time of writing this is not accessible) to a long woodland shaw where the fences finish. Walk along the right-hand side of this shaw until just before it ends, where you cut left among the trees, then immediately turn right. A few paces later come onto a track leading to a concrete farm road. Shortly after, bear left on a stony track known as Garden

Hill Lane (Grid ref: 633214). A small brook runs along this track, growing as the way progresses, until it becomes a proper stream.

This little brook brightened my day. So far the walk had been enjoyable in virtually every step, but the company of this fresh chalk stream was enough to raise my spirits even more. Why? It was a rarity on this walk, it is true, for chalk hills are reluctant to show their streams, yet here was one that had found escape and I rejoiced with it as I considered its progress through the hills: first as moisture seeping into the downland turf, draining by way of grass roots, the root systems of flowers and shrubs and trees into the multi-layers of unseen chalk, percolating through that soft, cheese-like rock, passing hard blocks of flint that one distant day will no doubt be exposed to the winds. Slowly, persistently, the moisture trickled and dripped through the bosom of the hills until it met with the sticky resistance of a clay bed. There, water was trapped until sufficient of it could force a means of escape. And this little brook announced that escape, that release to sunshine and fresh air, with a chuckle and a swirl among the stones.

Jogging from one side to the other a narrow pathway follows the stream among the trees. In places it is something of a tight squeeze and a rucksack can easily be snagged by low branches. And all the while the stream cuts its channel below. After ½ mile of this you come to the embankment of a dismantled railway which you cross and continue ahead.

Note: *If you plan to stay overnight in* **West Meon**, *turn right along the embankment and follow the one-time railway north-east for about 2 miles. A little over halfway along this track pass Hayden Farm on the outskirts of* **Warnford**. *At the time of writing both villages have accommodation and refreshments.*

When at last you leave the tree-lined, streamside path and come to a farm track, veer right, soon crossing a footbridge over the lovely River Meon. A few more paces brings you to the A32 on the outskirts of **Exton** (Grid ref: 618213). Cross over with care and take the minor road opposite into the village, bearing right to pass the church. To the left the lane leads to the village pub, *The Shoe*.

Note: *Walkers planning to find accommodation in **Corhampton** should head south a short distance along the A32.*

Exton (*refreshments*) is a pleasant village happily spared traffic from the A32 by standing a little to one side of the road. Its name suggests it was a farmstead of the East Saxons. The flint-walled parish church dates from the 13th century, and has a wooden belfry. The village pub lies just to the south among a second group of cottages.

Items of Interest:

1: Queen Elizabeth Country Park consists of 1400 acres of forest and downland which includes Butser Hill. Several waymarked walks explore the woods and Downs of the Park, including the 12 mile (19km) Staunton Way, a linear path which begins here, then heads south across the Downs to Staunton Country Park, and continues alongside the Hermitage Stream to Broadmarsh on Langstone Harbour. The Hangers Way is another linear route which heads north from the Park on a 21mile (34km) journey to Alton, passing through Buriton and Selborne along the way.

2: Butser Hill is the highest point on the South Downs, the site of ancient trackways, Bronze Age burial mounds, Celtic fields and defensive dykes. There is also evidence of Romano-British occupation. On the summit of the hill stands a beacon that would have been lit in times of danger or of celebration, but this is dwarfed by the unsightly telecommunications mast. From Butser Hill a justifiably renowned panorama attracts crowds of visitors on bright summer days.

3: East Meon is a pretty village with the River Meon, which rises nearby, running alongside the main street. Izaak Walton, who wrote *The Compleat Angler*, stayed here to fish the local river, and one of the two village pubs is named after him. The Norman church of All Saints overlooks the village from the foot of Park Hill, its green broach spire seen from far away. The Court House is said to be of the 15th century, and there are several attractive cottages in a subtle mix of colours, some of which date from the 18th century.

*East Meon, with the River Meon flowing through it,
lies just over a mile off the South Downs Way*

4: Old Winchester Hill was the site of Bronze Age burial barrows, and an Iron Age hill fort. The outline of the fort is clearly evident and covers an area of about 14 acres. Much of the hilltop and the nearby coomb is National Nature Reserve, covering 150 acres in all, and is rich with downland flora and butterflies.

SECTION 12: EXTON TO WINCHESTER

Distance:	**12 miles (19km)**
Maps:	**Harveys South Downs Way 1:40,000**
	OS Landranger 185 Winchester & Basingstoke Area 1:50,000
	OS Explorer 132 Winchester, New Alresford & East Meon 1:25,000
Accommodation:	**The Milburys (nr Beauworth) and Winchester**
Refreshments:	**The Milburys (nr Beauworth) and Winchester**

This final stage of the journey from Eastbourne provides an assortment of scenic pleasures. The landscape changes pattern by the hour as you travel through it, whilst the Way itself varies between footpath, bridleway, track and quiet country lane. Winchester remains hidden from view virtually until the very last field path, but the heart of this historic city makes a worthy finish to the South Downs Way.

On departing from Exton the route heads roughly north-westward climbing sharply to the nature reserve on Beacon Hill – yet another ancient site. From there you pass the (unseen) site of a lost village, cross the route of the Wayfarer's Walk and take to a series of near-empty country roads and green lanes before coming to Gander Down. This is a big open countryside, a spacious land of mellow hills and gentle valleys, but from it another green lane takes you into and alongside woodlands as far as Cheesefoot Head. The end of the journey is near, but there is one last stretch of downland to cover before descending from the escarpment through a sunken lane leading to tiny Chilcomb, and from there across one final field and the M3, into the streets of Winchester.

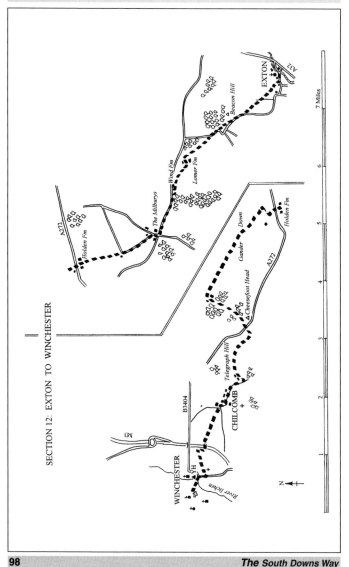

SECTION 12: EXTON TO WINCHESTER

With Exton parish church on your right walk along the lane which curves leftwards, then break away to the right along a track opposite a flint wall. The track cuts between Glebe Cottage and Bramcote House, and leads to a stile next to a field gate. Over this walk directly ahead to a second stile (on the right), then cross the next field to the far left corner. Maintain direction to reach a farm track, and continue ahead, now crossing the near right-hand corner of the next field to locate a stile near a water trough.

Once again maintain direction to a woodland shaw and yet another stile, over which the path climbs steeply, then across the right-hand corner of a sloping field to a stile found about 30 yards up the slope. In the final steep hillside meadow the path is sometimes rather vague on the ground, in which case the direction to make for is the top right-hand corner where a footpath signpost stands beside a stile leading to a country lane (Grid ref: 603221).

Turn right along the lane for about 500 yards then, a little west of **Beacon Hill**,[1] cross a stile in the right-hand hedge and take a path striking half-left to the far corner of the field. There you come to a parking area at Beaconhill Beeches where the **bridleway and foot-path routes rejoin** (Grid ref: 598227).

On leaving the car park area go ahead along the lane for almost 300 yards, with woodland to your right, then as the lane curves right, continue ahead along a farm track. A short distance beyond Lomer Cottage a few grassy mounds may be detected off to the left – all that remains of the village of Lomer which, though mentioned in the Domesday Book, died out in the Middle Ages. This is one of 90 such 'lost villages' of Hampshire. A little over ½ mile from the lane you come to **Lomer Farm**. Bear left by some barns, then turn right immediately after passing farm cottages. The way bears left along another track which leads through arable farmland for more than half a mile to **Wind Farm**, and is shared by the route of the Wayfarers Walk.[2] The track can be very muddy following wet weather.

Wind Farm stands on the edge of woodlands, and with a minor road running by. Bear right to the road and then turn left along it for about ¾ mile. There is a path, of sorts, on the right-hand side. On the left is Millbarrow Down, and a burial mound not far from the road is known as Mill Barrow. A windmill once stood on this Bronze Age site.

At a crossroads turn right and in a few paces you come to **The Milburys** pub (*accommodation, also camping, refreshments*). Take the next road on the left after the pub, signposted to High Stoke, a peaceful Hampshire lane ideal for cyclists. When it makes a right-hand bend near a Dutch barn, leave the road and continue straight ahead on a farm track known as Holden lane – another true green lane which leads for almost a mile through pleasant countryside, passes **Holden Farm** and comes to the A272 Petersfield to Winchester road (Grid ref: 561269).

Cross the road with care and continue ahead on a short, tree-lined track which brings you to a field gate. Through this the bridleway bears right to follow the boundary hedge, but a notice offers walkers the option (unless crops are growing) of cutting through the meadow to the far right-hand corner. In the first corner the bridleway route turns left with the hedge, and eventually comes to a bridle gate in the top corner. Ganderdown Farm huddles below to the left, while ahead stretches the broad rolling countryside of **Gander Down**, a breezy open landscape of big skies and unfolding panoramas. Through the gate the way continues beneath power lines and joins a clear, hedge-lined track aiming north-west.

My walk was drawing to a close, but I was strangely reluctant to finish. Around me the countryside spread in breeze-blown splendour. Peewits wheeled and cried and swooped one over another, gusting and playful, yet mournful too with their sorrowing cry. Coming to a barn stocked with straw bales I settled myself out of the wind to eat my sandwiches and let the miles since Eastbourne shuffle themselves in my mind. It had been a grand walk – it still was – and my love for the ever-varied landscapes of Britain had grown stronger with each succeeding day. Now I stretched out in comfort and watched a puff of raincloud sweep my way. 'Precipitation in sight', as they say on the shipping forecast. It came, dampened the track, rattled on the barn roof, and was gone again. Sunshine took over. A hare loped along the track and confronted a cock pheasant only a few feet from where I sat. They stared at each other, then carried on with their own business, totally unaware that I was watching. The cock bird then caught sight of something of interest and strutted away, head projecting like a Victorian spinster scurrying off to Mattins. Five minutes later a hen pheasant emerged from the adjacent field through an open gateway, and stood looking for her mate, squinting up and down. I was tempted to tell her where he'd gone, but decided to remain incognito and let the natural world continue around me, undisturbed by my presence. After all, who was I to interfere?

The track crosses Rodfield Lane and maintains direction for a further 1¼ miles until reaching crosstracks at a group of farm buildings. Bear left to pass the flint-walled Keeper's Cottage (barns on the right), and continue through woods on a clear trail. Beyond the woods follow a hedge-line, then through a bridle gate to an enclosed path along a splendid avenue of beech trees with Great Clump Woods to the left. Eventually arrive beside the A272 at **Cheesefoot Head**.[3]

Across the road another bridleway leads through a field for about 100 yards to a path junction. Turn right among trees and scrub to an enclosed continuing track. Approaching **Telegraph Hill**'s tumulus the way leads between a plantation on the left and a field on the right, beyond which it curves leftward and reaches a crossing track (Grid ref: 517281). Turn left and follow this to Little Golders and a narrow metalled lane where you turn right to slope downhill between high banks. The lane leads to the hamlet of Chilcomb, the last habitation before Winchester. As you enter **Chilcomb** note the black-timbered grain store on staddle stones seen across a hedge on the right.

At a road junction bear right beside a flint wall. (The rather fine Saxon church of Chilcomb stands at the end of the left-hand lane.) A few yards later come to a Y-shaped road junction with a few steps leading to a stile directly opposite.

Note: *The way ahead is for walkers only. The bridleway route turns right here along Kings Lane, then left on A31 to gain Winchester by road. This is another 'temporary' route – watch for signs and notices.*

Cross the stile and walk alongside the very last field, with Winchester now in view ahead. On the far side of the field bear left through scrub to cross the M3 by footbridge, then swing right on the tarmac path along the outer edge of town. At an obvious T-junction of paths turn left alongside trees, so to reach Petersfield Road. Walk straight ahead, eventually passing All Saints Church on the left, and slope downhill, where Petersfield Road becomes East Hill and shortly after comes to a crossroads. Turn right into Chesil Street. At a round-about bear left into the High Street (the youth hostel is off to the right in Water Lane), and cross the bridge over the River Itchen to King Alfred's statue. Continue ahead into the main shopping area, then left where signs indicate, to reach **Winchester** Cathedral – a fitting climax to the South Downs Way.

Winchester (*accommodation, refreshments*) was the Saxon capital of England, but is now very much a small city wrestling to find harmony between the old and the new. There is much of interest – historically, architecturally, spiritually. There is the famous College, founded in 1382; the Pilgrims Hall where pilgrims stayed on their way to Canterbury; the fine old City Mill (built 1774, owned by the National Trust and leased to YHA as a youth hostel); the lovely houses, archways, castle ruins, the Hospital of the Holy Cross. But the cathedral is the most obvious, for this is the very heart and soul of Winchester. Graceful, and at the same time, a little severe on the outside, the interior is astonishingly beautiful. Sit there at the end of the long walk and absorb the calm whispering glory that hangs in the air. The building was started in 1079 on the site of an earlier Saxon church built by King Alfred, but it was not completed until 1404, and clearly belongs to many different periods of history. Each era added something inimitable. Today Winchester is one of Europe's longest cathedrals at 556ft/170m. But it is more than that. Enter its peaceful sanctuary and be thankful for all the days of your journey along the South Downs. (Tourist Information Centre: The Guildhall, The Broadway, Winchester, Hants SO23 9LJ ☎ 01962 840500.)

Items of Interest:

1: Beacon Hill is yet another Iron Age hill fort site with hut circles in evidence, and signs of agricultural workings. There is also a cause-wayed ditch considered even older than the hill fort – Neolithic, perhaps? The summit of Beacon Hill is a National Nature Reserve with no less than 13 species of wild orchid growing there.

2: The Wayfarers Walk is a 70 mile (113km) long distance walk developed in 1981 by Hampshire County Council. It begins at Emsworth Marina and finishes at Inkpen Beacon on the Hampshire–Berkshire border, crossing on the way Walbury Camp, at 974ft (297m) the highest chalk hill in southern Britain. The South Downs Way is crossed between Lomer Farm and Wind Farm.

3: Cheesefoot Head east of Winchester makes a natural amphitheatre, and is where General Eisenhower addressed the Allied troops in 1944 in advance of the D-Day landings.

APPENDIX A: USEFUL ADDRESSES

1: Countryside Agency
   South-East Regional Office
   71 Kingsway
   LONDON WC2B 6ST

2: East Sussex County Council
   Rights of Way & Countryside Management
   Sackville House
   Brooks Road
   LEWES
   East Sussex BN7 1EU (☎ 01273 482670)

3: Hampshire County Council
   Rights of Way Section
   Countryside Planning Department
   Mottisfont Court
   WINCHESTER
   Hants SO23 8ZF (☎ 01962 846045)

4: The Ramblers' Association
   1/5 Wandsworth Road
   LONDON SW8 2XX (☎ 020 7339 8500)

5: Society of Sussex Downsmen
   93 Church Road
   HOVE
   East Sussex BN3 2BA

6: South Downs Way Officer
   Sussex Downs Conservation Board
   Stanmer Park
   Lewes Road
   BRIGHTON
   East Sussex BN1 9SE (☎ 01273 625242)

7: South-East England Tourist Board
    The Old Brew House
    Warwick Park
    TUNBRIDGE WELLS
    Kent TN2 5TU (☎ 01892 540766)

8: Southern England Tourist Board
    40 Chamberlayne Road
    EASTLEIGH
    Hampshire SO5 5JH

9: Sussex Downs Conservation Board
    Chanctonbury House
    Church Street
    STORRINGTON
    West Sussex RH20 4LT (☎ 01903 741234)

10: West Sussex County Council
    Countryside Management Unit
    Planning Department
    County Hall
    CHICHESTER
    West Sussex PO19 1RQ (☎ 01243 777610)

11: Youth Hostels Association (England & Wales)
    8 St Stephen's Hill
    ST ALBANS
    Herts AL1 2DY (☎ 0870 870 8808)

12: Stilwell Publishing Ltd
    59 Charlotte Road
    Shoreditch
    LONDON EC2A 3QT (☎ 020 7739 7179)

APPENDIX B: PUBLIC TRANSPORT INFORMATION

1: Connex South Central Trains
   (serving stations on or near the SDW)
   Timetable info: (☎ 0845 748 4950)

2: East Sussex Public Transport Helpline
   (Mon–Fri 9am–1pm, 2–4pm) (☎ 01273 474747)

3: Hampshire County Surveyors Department
   The Castle
   WINCHESTER
   Hants SO22 8UJ

4: West Sussex Traveline (daily, 7am–8pm) (☎ 0345 959099)

APPENDIX C: RECOMMENDED READING

	Illustrated Guide to Britain (AA/Drive Publications)
Armstrong, R	*A History of Sussex* (Phillimore)
Baker, M	*Sussex Villages* (Robert Hale)
Brandon, P	*The South Saxons* (Phillimore)
	The Sussex Lancscape (Hodder & Stoughton)
	Sussex (Making of the English Landscape series, Hodder & Stoughton)
Darby, B	*South Downs* (Robert Hale)
	View of Sussex (Robert Hale)
Godfrey, J	*Sussex* (New Shell Guides series, Michael Joseph)
Harrison, D	*Along the South Downs Way* (Cassell)
Hillier, C & Mosley, J	*Images of the Downs* (McMillan)
Hudson, WH	*Nature in Downland* (London)
Jebb, M	*A Guide to the South Downs Way* (Constable)
Jefferies, R	*Nature Near London* (John Clare Books)
Mason, O	*South-East England* (Bartholomew)
Millmore, P	*South Downs Way* (Aurum Press)
Moore, C	*Green Roof of Sussex* (Middleton Press)
O'Dell, N	*Portrait of Hampshire* (Robert Hale)
Perkins, B	*South Downs Way for Motorists* (Frederick Warne)
Pyatt, EC	*Chalkways of South and South-East England* (David & Charles)
Reynolds, K	*Walking in Sussex* (Cicerone Press)
	Classic Walks in Southern England (Oxford Illustrated Press)
Sankey, J	*Nature Guide to South-East England* (Usborne)
Scholes, R	*Understanding the Countryside* (Moorland Publishing)
Spence, K	*The Companion Guide to Kent & Sussex* (Collins)
White, JT	*The South-East, Down and Weald* (Eyre-Methuen)
Woodford, C	*Portrait of Sussex* (Robert Hale)

CICERONE GUIDES

SOUTH AND SOUTH-WEST LONG DISTANCE TRAILS

THE KENNET & AVON WALK   *Ray Quinlan*
90 miles along riverside and canal, from Westminster to Avonmouth, full of history, wildlife, delectable villages and pubs.
ISBN 1 85284 090 0 200pp

THE LEA VALLEY WALK   *Leigh Hatts*
Split into 20 stages this 50 mile walk is one of the finest and most varied walking routes around the capital, tracing the route of the River Lea from the Millennium Dome to its source.
ISBN 1 85284 313 6 128pp

THE NORTH DOWNS WAY   *Kev Reynolds*
The North Downs Way runs west from Farnham to Dover. The routes are each split into 12 day sections, with advice on stopping points.

THE SOUTHERN COAST-TO-COAST WALK   *Ray Quinlan*
The equivalent of the popular northern walk. 283 miles from Weston-super-Mare to Dover.
ISBN 1 85284 117 6 200pp

SOUTH WEST WAY - A Walker's Guide to the Coast Path   *Martin Collins*
Vol.1: Minehead to Penzance
ISBN 1 85284 025 0 184pp PVC cover

Vol.2: Penzance to Poole
ISBN 1 85284 026 9 198pp PVC cover
Two volumes which cover the spectacular 560 mile coastal path around Britain's south-west peninsula. Profusely illustrated and filled with practical details.

THE THAMES PATH   *Leigh Hatts*
From the Thames Barrier to the source. This popular guide provides all the information needed to complete this delightful scenic route. 180 miles in 20 stages.
ISBN 1 85284 270 9 184pp

THE TWO MOORS WAY   *James Roberts*
100 miles crossing Dartmoor the delightful villages of central Devon and Exmoor to the rugged coast at Lynmouth.
ISBN 1 85284 159 1 100pp £5.99

THE WEALDWAY AND THE VANGUARD WAY   *Kev Reynolds*
Two long distance walks, from the outskirts of London to the south coast. The 81 mile Wealdway runs from Gravesend to Beachy Head, while the 62 mile Vanguard Way goes from Croydon to Seaford Head in Sussex.
ISBN 0 902363 85 9` 160pp

SOUTHERN AND SOUTH-EAST ENGLAND

CANAL WALKS Vol 3: South   *Dennis Needham*
ISBN 1 85284 227 X 176pp

WALKING IN BEDFORDSHIRE   *Alan Castle*
32 fascinating walks of short and medium length for all abilities and interests. Maps and details of local interest abound.
ISBN 1 85284 312 8

WALKING IN BUCKINGHAMSHIRE *Robert Wilson*
32 walks through bluebell woods, rolling Chiltern hills and pretty villages. The walks are of short and medium length for all abilities and interests, including sections of Icknield Way.
ISBN 1 85284 301 2

WALKING IN THE CHILTERNS *Duncan Unsworth*
35 short circular walks in this area of woods and little valleys with cosy pubs and old churches.
ISBN 1 85284 127 3 184pp

WALKING IN HAMPSHIRE *David Foster and Nick Chandler*
With a range of landscapes from coastal beaches and marsh, downlands, river valleys and the New Forest, this county offers exceptional beauty. Delightful walks of short and medium length.
ISBN 1 85284 311 X

A WALKER'S GUIDE TO THE ISLE OF WIGHT *Martin Collins & Norman Birch*
The best walks on this sunshine island, including short circuits and longer trails.
ISBN 1 85284 221 0 216 pp

WALKING IN KENT: Vol I *Kev Reynolds*
ISBN 1 85284 192 3 200pp

WALKING IN KENT: Vol II *Kev Reynolds*
ISBN 1 85284 156 7 200pp
Two books which cover the best of walking in the county.

LONDON THEME WALKS *Frank Duerden*
Ten fascinating walks based on popular themes.
ISBN 1 85284 145 1 144pp

RURAL RIDES No.1: WEST SURREY
ISBN 1 85284 272 5 192pp

RURAL RIDES No.2: EAST SURREY
ISBN 1 85284 273 3 160pp *Ron Strutt*

WALKING IN SUSSEX *Kev Reynolds*
40 walks in the great variety of scenery and history of Sussex. Short walks and more demanding routes, including outline descriptions of some of the region's long distance paths.
ISBN 1 85284 292 X 240pp

SOUTH-WEST ENGLAND

CHANNEL ISLAND WALKS *Paddy Dillon*
47 one-day walks in this wonderful holiday area, with easy bus and boat services. Walks on Jersey, Guernsey, Alderney, Sark and Herm.
ISBN 1 85284 288 1

CORNISH ROCK *Rowland Edwards & Tim Dennell*
A superb photo topo guide to West Penwith, the most popular climbing in Cornwall, by the area's leading activists.
ISBN 1 85284 208 3 234pp A5 size Casebound

WALKING IN CORNWALL *John Earle*
30 walks including the Coast Path and the interesting interior.
ISBN 1 85284 217 2 200pp

WALKING ON DARTMOOR *John Earle*
The most comprehensive walking guide to the National Park. Includes 43 walks and outlines 4 longer walks.
ISBN 0 902363 84 0 224pp

WALKING IN DEVON   *David Woodthorpe*
16 coastal, 15 countryside and 14 Dartmoor walks.
ISBN 1 85284 223 7 200pp

WALKING IN DORSET   *James Roberts*
Circular walks between 5 and 12 miles in a rich variety of scene. Spectacular coastline, lovely downs and fine pubs.
ISBN 1 85284 180 X 232pp

A WALKER'S GUIDE TO THE PUBS OF DARTMOOR
Chris Wilson & Michael Bennie
60 Dartmoor inns. Everything a walker needs to know.
ISBN 1 85284 115 X 152 pp

EXMOOR AND THE QUANTOCKS   *John Earle*
Walks for all the family on the moors, valleys and coastline.
ISBN 1 85284 083 8 200pp

WALKING IN THE ISLES OF SCILLY   *Paddy Dillon*
With its mild climate and relaxing atmosphere, this is an ideal retreat. Walks and boat trips are described, with stunning scenery and beautiful plants and flowers.
ISBN 1 85284 310 1

WALKING IN SOMERSET   *James Roberts*
Walks between 3 and 12 miles, gentle rambles to strenuous hikes, on Exmoor, the Quantocks and the pastoral lowlands.
ISBN 1 85284 253 9 280pp

THE MIDLANDS

CANAL WALKS Vol: 2 Midlands   *Dennis Needham*
ISBN 1 85284 225 3 176pp

TWENTY COTSWOLD TOWNS   *Clive Holmes*
Clive describes and draws the most interesting features of these attractive towns.
ISBN 1 85284 249 0 144pp A4 Case bound

THE COTSWOLD WAY   *Kev Reynolds*
A glorious walk of 102 miles along high scarp edges, through woodlands and magical villages by one of Britain's best guide writers.
ISBN 1 85284 049 8 168pp

COTSWOLD WALKS (3 volumes)   *Clive Holmes*
60 walks of between 1 and 10 miles, with local points of interest explained. Beautifully illustrated.
ISBN 1 85284 139 7 (North) 144pp
ISBN 1 85284 140 0 (Central) 160pp
ISBN 1 85284 141 9 (South) 144pp

THE GRAND UNION CANAL WALK   *Clive Holmes*
13 easy stages along the canal which links the Black Country to London. Delightful illustrations.
ISBN 1 85284 206 7 128pp

AN OXBRIDGE WALK   *J.A. Lyons*
Over 100 miles linking the university cities of Oxford and Cambridge. Generally undemanding and easy to follow.
ISBN 1 85284 166 4 168pp

WALKING IN OXFORDSHIRE   *Leslie Tomlinson*
36 walks from all parts of the county, and suitable for all the family.
ISBN 1 85284 244 X 200pp